I Am Come To Bring Living Water

by
Darris L. Martin

Larger Print Version

I Am Come To Bring Living Water

I Am Come To Bring Living Water

Printed in the United States of America

First Printing: March 2011

ISBN- 978-0-9833992-2-3

Larger Print Version

I Am Come To Bring Living Water

Larger Print Version

I Am Come To Bring Living Water

I Am One Track

I am the bearer of Living Water. I am come to bring Living Water. The grass of a field, the lily of a valley and people will dry up and die without water. How much more so will your soul parish without the Living Water of life. I am not the creator of the Living Water and I am not the Living Water. I am just the bearer of the Living Water.

But whosoever drinketh of the water that I shall give him shall never thirst: but the water that I shall give him shall be in him a well of water springing up into everlasting life. (John 4:14)

I had a home with two beautiful window seal flower pots. They were located on each side of the living room, which protruded out from the front of the home. I planted multi-colored flowers seeds in each pot and watch them grow into an over stuffing of wonderful flowers. But soon afterwards, the flowers collapsed and turned brown. I looked at the pots thinking once again I had failed to have a green thumb others displayed so lovely in their yards. But God allowed me to notice the pots were not catching any rain water because they were under the overhang of the roof. So I watered the flowers. In fact, I over watered the flowers until the water was almost leafing out of the top of the pots. The next day I had the most beautiful flowers again. For the rest of the summer, when the flowers collapsed, I just added water and they spring to life. Christian life is also just that easy to ignite. All it takes is a drink of Living Water. This water you only have to provide once and it will last a life time. In fact Living Water will last an eternity.

Christian church congregations are becoming very dried up and deadly. When you walk in some Christian churches, you really began to understand what God meant by "Prophesy upon these bones" in Ezekiel 37:4. Some say the Christian church dryness is a form of reverence. They define reverence as quiet, respectable, and humble, but mostly quiet. If a football or basketball game was this quiet, few would watch. Maybe that is why fewer and fewer people are attending Christian church services. You really could stay at home and get just as much value out of watching a TV church service. Maybe watching Christian TV offers move value than the Christian church since it is a little livelier.

Reverence is not defined as being quiet. Silent is not a required element of respect and it does not describe worship. Reverence is being at awe and showing admiration. What may have caused the silent quietness in the Christian churches were parents telling children to be quiet in the church in the presence of God. Children believed sitting and saying nothing was how one worshipped God, but what parents really wanted was to stop the worship of everything other than God by means of non Godly conversation in the church.

Christian churches should not be deadly. Christians should not be dead. We believe in a Christ that is rose from the dead and is alive today, so we too should not be deadly. I can say we ought to be alive over and over again in the Christian church and all at once it will wake up and seem alive. But a few days later, like the next Sunday, it is deadly again. As you read these words, your interest may be peaking. You may even be responding with a lively feeling. But what is lacking is the way to sustain the feeling. You may need a way to awaken and remain awake. You may need a formula, a pill, or something to keep going. It like using peep drinks and peep pills. You may need something like a peep drink or pill, but it has to be the Christian kind. What you may need is a drink of Living Water. Not a two or five hour pick-up kind, but a kind that lasts an entire life time and takes you into eternity.

When Jesus went to villages and synagogues, he did more than teach. He also healed all manner of sickness and disease. The same thing happen when his disciple visited villages and synagogues after his resurrection. When was the last time you saw a healing miracle? Somewhere along the way after Jesus' resurrection, some Christians just decided it was not necessary to work miracles. Some Christians decided miracles were no longer a part of the Christian ministry. Well I disagree. I think many

I Am Come To Bring Living Water

Christians somehow got onto the wrong road. I think a few Christians began to settle for something less than what Jesus offered. Some started drying up like a flower not getting enough water. Many Christians got Jesus, but did not wait around to get the Living Water. If those Christians had it, they probably would not seem so dried up and the miracles most likely would still be witnessed. And since you only need to drink once to never thirst again, then many Christians must have never gotten the Living Water.

> *And Jesus went about all Galilee, teaching in the synagogues, and preaching the gospel of the kingdom, and healing all manner of sickness and all manner of disease among the people. And his fame went throughout all Syria: and they brought unto him all sick people that were taken with divers diseases and torments, and those which were possessed with devils, and those that had the palsy; and he healed them. And there followed him great multitudes of people from Galilee, and from Decapolis, and from Jerusalem, and from Judaea, and from beyond Jordan. (Matt. 4:23-25)*

This is the miraculous experience I need in my daily Christian walk. With this type of experience, wining souls for Christ becomes as it was in Christ's day. The multitudes would come and they would be changed by their conviction to Jesus. I know several great bible scholars and many Christian leaders say this is foolish. Many will state, people do not need signs and wonders to believe in Jesus. And those may go on stating furthermore, a person is more blessed when there are no signs and wonders and they believe in Jesus from just hearing the word of God. That is true, but what is wrong with a miracle every now and then to reach those that will not believe without signs and wonders.

In times of good economical health, few notice the need for miraculous divine intervention in life. But with a down turned economy, people trying to decide if they should buy medicine or food, and everyone trying to find better ways to get more out of every dollar spent, most people need a Savior. That is when most Christians notice the need for a few miracles.

I Am Come To Bring Living Water

It sounds like I linked miracles to Living Water. Well I did. I for one do not like the reality I live with in this world. I have to stay in this world until Christ calls me home, so I am going to try to change my reality in this world. I am going to use the things Jesus gave me to create a new reality (liken unto the Kingdom of God). Living Water is one of those things I will use to enter my new reality (the Kingdom of God). Living Water came from God by Jesus. It was not mentioned as a gift from God to mankind before Jesus went to Jacob's well when he needed to go through Samaria. In all of the time from the beginning in Genesis, through Moses, David and all the prophets of old, no one gave mankind Living Water. Solomon spoke of Living Water as

A fountain of gardens, a well of living waters, and streams from Lebanon. (Song of Songs 4:15)

Jeremiah spoke of Living Water and proclaimed God's people have sinned by forsaken the Lord of the fountains of Living Water in Jeremiah 17:13. And Zechariah prophesied about Living Waters going out from Jerusalem in Zechariah 14:8. Even John the Baptist, baptized in water, but did not give anyone Living Water. John talked about being given Living Water by the one following him that was to be before him, but John did not give anyone Living Water. When Christians are baptized today, do they get Living Water? Do most ministers understand how to give Living Water? Do they have any to give? Don't think badly of today's ministers, many before them did not have this Living Water to give either. Are Christians aware of the need to receive Living Water? And most important, did you get your drink of Living Water?

Many Christians think I am very one track. I am writing about Living Water as if it is the only thing Jesus gave to Christians. Well it is not the only thing Jesus gave Christians, but I am very one track. It is my calling. It is my job. It is my talent. If I were called to do something else I would be doing something else. But I am the bearer of Living Water. I am come to bring Living Water. The grass of a field, the lily of a valley and people will dry up and die without water. How much more so will your

I Am Come To Bring Living Water

soul parish without the Living Water of life. I am not the creator of the Living Water and I am not the Living Water. I am just the bearer of the Living Water.

And herein is that saying true, One soweth, and another reapeth. (John 4:37)

Someone has to water in between the sowing and reaping. Jesus left us with Living Water, but if Christianity is dying away and churches are failing for lack of membership, then someone did not get their Living Water. And I am come to bring Living Water.

And God hath set some in the church, first apostles, secondarily prophets, thirdly teachers, after that miracles, then gifts of healing, helps, governments, diversities of tongues. Are all apostles? Are all prophets? Are all teachers? Are all workers of miracles? Have all the gifts of healing? Do all speak in tongues? Do all interpret? (1 Cor. 12:27-30)

Yes I am one track. Others are responsible for the other tracks. I am just responsible for bringing the Living Water. I need to get Christians to drink Living Water.

I Am Called

A church in Greenville, Mississippi is where I started a forty plus year discovery of my true calling. Along the way I displayed many talents given to me by Christ, but I never understood or discovered the power of the most important talent given. All Christians have talents. They are not all the same and they are not always the ones that get the most fame. The talents we have are a gift from Christ and the full benefit of life in Christ (in the Kingdom of Heaven) is not realized until the talents are put to use.

For the kingdom of heaven is as a man travelling into a far country, who called his own servants, and delivered unto them his goods. And unto one he gave five talents, to another two, and to another one; to every man according to his several ability; and straightway took his journey. Then he that had received the five talents went and traded with the same, and made them other five talents. And likewise he that had received two, he also gained other two. But he that had received one went and digged in the earth, and hid his lord's money. After a long time the lord of those servants cometh, and reckoneth with them. And so he that had received five talents came and brought other five talents, saying, Lord, thou deliveredst unto me five talents: behold, I have gained beside them five talents more. His lord said unto him, Well done, thou good and faithful servant: thou hast been faithful over a few things, I will make thee ruler over many things: enter thou into the joy of thy lord. He also that had received two talents came and said, Lord, thou deliveredst unto me two talents: behold, I have gained two other talents beside them. His lord said unto him, Well done, good and faithful servant; thou hast been faithful over a few things, I will make thee ruler over many things: enter thou into the joy of thy lord. Then he which had received the one talent came and said, Lord, I knew thee that thou art an hard man, reaping where thou hast not sown, and gathering where thou hast not strawed: And I was afraid, and went and hid thy talent in the earth: lo, there thou hast that is thine. His lord answered and said unto him, Thou wicked and slothful servant, thou knewest that I reap where I sowed not, and gather where I have not strawed: Thou oughtest therefore to have put my money to the exchangers, and then at my coming I should have received mine own with usury. Take therefore the talent from him, and give it unto him which hath ten talents. For unto every one that hath shall be given, and he shall have abundance: but from him that hath not shall be taken away even that which he hath. (Matt. 25:14-25)

I first received my most valuable talent at that church in Greenville Mississippi. Putting that talent to work is my true life calling. It took me over forty years to understand what Christ gave me. I was just a little boy with very little knowledge of Jesus. All I knew about Jesus was what I had been told by my parents and teachers.

The church in Greenville, Mississippi was a magnificent structure. It was so beautiful people visiting the city would stop to take pictures. With large stained windows (more than 20 feet wide and 30 feet high) on each side of the church it was a site to behold. It was build before the great flood of 1927 and it was well build. It survived the flood waters. It was built several feet above the ground on a foundation similar to stilts or pylons. What a wonderful way to survive a flood, being safely above the water. It is as if God had instructed them to build an ark. Just think about the wonder and power of God to direct his children to build a church high above the ground to be safe from a flood to come in the future. A flood none of the saints at the time could have known about. Before 1927, the water never flooded that high or came pass the boundary of the levee. In prior years and for a little while even in 1927, Greenville always considered itself as safe from floods because it was built away from a bend in the river with a lake between the city and the river. But in 1927, the backwaters of the river from a downstream break in the levee flooded the entire city with waters as high as roof tops.

I Am Come To Bring Living Water

I still remember the Sunday I felt a desire to come to Jesus. I was seated near the back of the church where most of us little ones hide to act disobedient in church services. I remember the prayer I prayed. I say Lord, I will make the first step into the isle, but you will have to help me make the next steps. And he has been helping me make the next steps since that day.

My next memory of those events was my baptism. I remember being in the water of the pool in church. I remember coming up out of the water and that is when my life changed and I got a gift that would take me more than forty years to understand. That is when I was first called. It was when Christ first touched me. I have been called and touch by Christ many times since, but that was the first and it was very special. I came up out of the water and two people, one on the left and one on the right took my arms and lifting me out of the water and out of the pool. I remember going across the church choir stand and back across the other way between the pulpit and the church congregation to get to the Pastor's study where a small rest room was located in which the men changed into and out of baptismal clothes. But most dramatically, I remember in that walk of more than 50 feet, I never touched the floor. I was carried by the two people, one on each arm. When you are caught up in the spirit, it is as if your soul is no longer in the world. It is as if your feet can no longer touch the reality of the sinful world in which we live. You are spiritually lifted up above the realm of this world. You are in the realm of the Kingdom of God.

Later that day, I asked my family at dinner, who lifted me out of the pool and carried me to the Pastor's study? My mother said no one carried you. You walked to the study by yourself. I insisted I was carried. My father, mother, brothers and sister all said I walked by myself. I still insisted I was carried. Finally, my grandmother said, no he is right. He was carried by two angles and I saw them too. Well that put a stop to dinner talk for the rest of the dinner. My grandmother pulled me aside a couple days later and tried to explain what had happened. But I was a child and not ready to hear the call of Jesus, understand his touch or its meaning in my life. This was the first time I had contact with Living Water. It happened in a church that with stood the great flood of 1927, remained standing and allowed the angles of God to lift me out of the world and into the Living Waters of Christ in the Kingdom of God. For those moments, I went to another place. It is a place not made by the hands of man. It is a place where Christ rules and reigns. It is the Kingdom of God. And I did not have to die and go to heaven to get there. It is right here and right at hand. To get to that place today I just needed to allow the Living Water that has been in me since my baptism to take me into the Kingdom of God.

Years later, while living in Louisville, Kentucky, I had a second experience with Living Water. I was a typical lukewarm Christian at the time.

So then because thou art lukewarm, and neither cold nor hot, I will spue thee out of my mouth. (Revelation 3:16)

I attended Church frequently (several times a week). I was a leader in the church. In fact I was a Sunday School superintendent in a large Church. On any giving Sunday, we had 150 to 200 attendees in Sunday school classes. I had become a great and well known bible teacher in the area churches. I also directed a small choir in the church. So why do I think I was lukewarm? I was missing the Holy Spirit in my life. I was a baptized Christian, but I did not know anything about the Holy Spirit. To me it was just a good feeling that you sometimes got when you hear the right song in church.

But Jesus was taking me on a journey. It was a journey that would educate me in the Word and fill me with the Holy Spirit. It was a journey that took several years and led me hundreds of miles away from Louisville to a bible school that grounded me in Christ. At the start of the journey, I was a young man with a real zeal for a Christian life. At the end, I was a fully called and ordained minister.

I completed college in Bloomington, Indiana. I attended the local church while in college. In my last year of school, I directed the church choir. The choir members were all college students and at the time being in the choir was just the fun thing to do. I finished college and started my work career in Bloomington, Indiana working for a very large corporation. I was transferred to Louisville by the corporation after a very short period in Bloomington, Indiana.

More out of habit than anything else, I quickly joined a church in Louisville to continue my practice of going to church each Sunday. Well it was not very long before the pastor started assigning me various responsibilities in the church. The one that was the most shocking was being named the superintendent of the Sunday School. I knew what the job was about, but performing the job was a learning experience for a very young Christian man.

God knew what he was doing in giving me that position. Prior to that day, I only studied the bible while in church. Sure I had one at home, but there was never a need to open it. In fact, it was still in the plastic rap it was in when my sister gave it to me as a gift years earlier. Since the pastor started teaching me and I had to start teaching the Sunday School teachers, I had to start reading my bible. For the next few years, this education of me in the Word continued in full progress.

In fact, since this was such a large Sunday School, I found myself actively involved in the ministry of growing the Sunday School. On Saturdays, some of the Sunday School leaders would join me going into the streets, house to house to seek new attendees for our Sunday School bus ministry. New buses required new attendees from new areas of the city. We worked hard and Church was a major part of my life.

Surprisingly to me, I was gaining a great love for the Word of God. My studies began to grow beyond just knowing enough to teach the teachers and to review the lesson highlights once a week. I began to want more.

My drive between home and church was half way across Louisville. It took at least thirty minutes each way on good traffic days. One night on the way home, I found a very unusual radio broadcast of a minister from Bradenton, Florida. The minister was originally from the Mennonite Church, but he was very good. He was teaching something about the Kingdom of God and I immediately wanted to know why I had never read the scriptures he spoke about the way he read them. It was like I had never really read those scriptures at all.

I began that night to re-study those same scriptures. In fact I studied everything I could find in the New Testament on Kingdom of God or Kingdom of Heaven. I order books written by the minister I heard on the radio. I read and studied the books and that is when I came to the realization I was missing something in my Christian walk. I had heard people mention what I was missing. I had even read about what I was missing in the bible. But I had not experience what I both heard and read.

I was missing the guidance of the Holy Spirit in my life. I needed to be baptized in the Holy Spirit. All at once, I recalled my childhood experience of coming up out the water in baptism and being lifted by two angels, one on the left and one on the right. I knew at once they were trying to guide me to something. The angels were trying to guide me to something more than my church had to offer. The angels were trying to guide me to the experience of being baptize in the Holy Ghost. The angels were leading me to experience the Holy Spirit descending like a dove into my life.

And Jesus, when he was baptized, went up straightway out of the water: and, lo, the heavens were opened unto him, and he saw the Spirit of God descending like a dove, and lighting upon him: (Matthew 3:16)

I began at once praying I receive the Holy Spirit. I did not fully understand what I was requesting. I did not have a saint that understood standing by to guide me into a baptism of the Holy Spirit. All I had was what I heard and read from the minister in Florida, the Word of God, and the presence of Jesus to guide me. I prayed for the baptism in the Holy Spirit for the next two weeks.

Once again on the long drive from church to home on a Wednesday night after prayer meeting and bible study, I was in the car listen to the minister from Florida. He talked about being baptized in the Holy Spirit and obtaining a heavenly language that allow you to talk to God and express needs even you did not understand.

For if I pray in an unknown tongue, my spirit prayeth, but my understanding is unfruitful. (1 Corinthians 14:14)

Likewise the Spirit also helpeth our infirmities: for we know not what we should pray for as we ought: but the Spirit itself maketh intercession for us with groanings which cannot be uttered. (Romans 8:26)

He said the heavenly language came with the baptism of the Holy Ghost. He said the language was gift of the Comforter Christ had promised to give to his disciples. He also talked about many other gifts of the Holy Spirit.

Now ye are the body of Christ, and members in particular. And God hath set some in the church, first apostles, secondarily prophets, thirdly teachers, after that miracles, then gifts of healings, helps, governments, diversities of tongues. (1 Corinthians 12:27-28)

As the broadcast ended, I began to pray for this baptism in the Holy Spirit while driving along in the car. I had just past the University of Louisville when God answered my prayer and allowed his Living Water (Holy Spirit) to fill my body. I all at once began to speak out loudly in the car words I did not understand. I had no understanding of where the sounds came from or how long they would last. But I rejoiced in the Lord, for my prayers were answered and I knew I had been baptized in the Holy Spirit. I was caught up in his Living Waters. The speaking in tongues lasted only about ten minutes. But the joy has lasted a life time. It is true, once you drink Living Waters, you never thirst again. I still rejoice over that moment in my life. Right then I decided somehow I was going to get to Florida and study more under the minister I heard on the radio. I did not know how, but I prophesied it would happen. The speaking in tongues was followed by more gifts and fruits of the spirit in my Christian walk.

Needless to say, I had a renewed zeal in church work from that day forward. Saints around me noticed and questioned what had happened. I shared the teachings of the minister from Florida and many received the same blessing of the baptism in the Holy Spirit (the Living Water) I received.

About two years later, the large corporation I worked for promoted me to a position in Daytona Beach, Florida. All I could think was I was getting closer to the minister I wanted to study under in Florida. Once again, I joined a local church and began teaching in the Sunday School after I moved to Florida. Many members were impressed by my teaching and help me start several small bible study classes in various homes of members. I joined a prayer group at work and I began attending a weekly prayer meeting at a Catholic church social hall late each Sunday night. It was at that prayer meeting I first heard of the Full Gospel Business Men's Fellowship in Daytona Beach.

I joined the Full Gospel Business Men's Fellowship in Daytona Beach and soon became their delegate to pray for sick members that were hospitalized. That small ministry resulted in years of being called at all hours to come and pray for the sick in a hospital. It was a very humbling ministry. What do you pray for when the family has said good bye, and the doctor is giving you a few minutes along with a saint just before they turn off the machine? What do you pray while you stand and watch the machine measuring the heart beat stop showing a heart beat? What do you pray when the doctor checks for a heart beat one last time and calls the time of death? What do you say to the family that is waiting in the lounge for you to come out of the intensive care room? I have had this experience. I have had it more times than I want to remember. I have witness more than my fare share of children of God crossing over before my eyes.

My heart is sore pained within me: and the terrors of death are fallen upon me. Fearfulness and trembling are come upon me, and horror hath overwhelmed me. And I said, Oh that I had wings like a dove! for then would I fly away, and be at rest. Lo, then would I wander far off, and remain in the wilderness. Selah. (Psalm 55:4-7)

Behold, I shew you a mystery; We shall not all sleep, but we shall all be changed, In a moment, in the twinkling of an eye, at the last trump: for the trumpet shall sound, and the dead shall be raised incorruptible, and we shall be changed. For this corruptible must put on incorruption, and this mortal must put on immortality. So when this corruptible shall have put on incorruption, and this mortal shall have put on immortality, then shall be brought to pass the saying that is written, Death is swallowed up in victory. O death, where is thy sting? O grave, where is thy victory? The sting of death is sin; and the strength of sin is the law. But thanks be to God, which giveth us the victory through our Lord Jesus Christ. (1 Corinthians 15:51-57)

The Saturday that started the fulfillment of prophesy finally came. The minister I listen to on the radio in Louisville was to be the speaker at the next Full Gospel Business Men's Fellowship Saturday prayer breakfast. It was a joyous morning. To hear in person the teachings of the Kingdom of God I had heard on the radio and read in books was almost too much for me to contain. I had told so many people about the experience in Louisville, that someone mentioned it to the minister. When I was introduced to him, he asked if I and several others would come to Bradenton, Florida and visit his church and Christian Retreat. A group of us visited the following week. We stay a few days. It was a wonderful place with several full time residents, a hotel, and a very large church. It was a place that praised God continuously. There were church services and classes each day and each evening. Even the birds on display in a large walk-in bird cage said, "Praise the Lord". In the service the last night I was there, that same minister I heard on the radio asked me to stand and he prophesied I would return to the Retreat as a student in his ministry school.

That is all it took. I had a job, a life, a career that was headed to the top of the large corporation, but I left it all. I left it all to follow my heart and Jesus. I had not moved to Florida to work for a corporation, but to go to the ministry school and start my ministry for Christ. I did just that. I quit my job and my life. I left everything with no concern of where the future would take me and I followed Christ. Everything I could not carry with me or put in storage, I gave away. I gave appliances, furniture and even money away and followed Christ against all of the negative warning I got from family, friends and my employer.

Jesus said unto him, If thou wilt be perfect, go and sell that thou hast, and give to the poor, and thou shalt have treasure in heaven: and come and follow me. (Matthew 19:21)

Signs And Wonders

Jesus often used signs and wonders to endorse his claim to be the Word of God.

And Jesus went about all Galilee, teaching in their syna-gogues, and preaching the gospel of the kingdom, and heal-ing all manner of sickness and all manner of disease among the people. And his fame went throughout all Syria: and they brought unto him all sick people that were taken with divers diseases and torments, and those which were possessed with devils, and those which were lunatick, and those that had the palsy; and he healed them. (Matthew 4:23-24)

His disciples were also given power to work signs and won-ders.

And he called unto him the twelve, and began to send them forth by two and two; and gave them power over unclean spirits; (Mark 6:7)

And even after the resurrection of Christ, his disciple and many other believers continued displaying signs and wonders in their ministry.

And they continued stedfastly in the apostles' doctrine and fellowship, and in breaking of bread, and in prayers. And fear came upon every soul: and many wonders and signs were done by the apostles. (Acts 2:42-43)

In many Christian churches of today, we have long since lost those signs and wonders. They are not a part of many ministries today. I have even heard bible teachers say the signs and won-ders were for a time when people would not believe without them and they are not needed for today. Well I disagree. Maybe there are so few people following Christ today because we no longer have the physical proof that Christ does exist. Maybe no one be-

16

lieves in the teaching of the Word of God because we offer no physical proof the Word we teach is the true Word of God. Maybe we no longer believe ourselves. It has become easier to discount the signs and wonders than to seek the power of God required to perform signs and wonders. The possession of gifts in signs and wonders requires application practice just like required for the possession of any other gift (such as learning to play a musical instrument).

I know the bible student will quickly remain me it is more blessed to not see and believe than to only believe if you see a sign or wonder. That is true, but sometimes, maybe when there is a need in the body of Christ, there should be a sign or a wonder. How can I minister the Word of God to a group of people that are in need of a miracle and leave without satisfying their need? Jesus did not teach that way and he did not tell his disciples to teach that way. Christ satisfied the needs of the people. He even did it when he knew the performance of those signs and wonders would cause the Pharisees to put him to death. After his resurrection, his disciples continued to satisfy the needs of the people. They also risk the possibility of death to satisfy the needs of the people. In fact, they appointed others to aid in the satisfaction of those needs.

So then you and I should have signs and wonders, yes even miracles in our ministering. I know I am called to bring Living Water. I know because I have witnessed the signs and wonders in my ministry that verify my calling. My only problem is it has taken me far too long to understand those signs and wonders. It has taken far too long to understand my calling.

The first time I witnessed the signs and wonders was over thirty years ago. It was not the first time God worked a miracle in my life for someone other than me, but it was the first time I pray for miracles to endorse my ministry and received a vision of what signs and wonders would happen so I would witness the fulfillment of my prayer just as I had envisioned. I was at the large church in Florida at Christian Retreat. I had been requested to teach a class for the ministry school students. It was a morning class rather than the more prestige evening services. God just has a way of taking the least expected at the least expected time and making it the most unexpected.

> *Jesus saith unto them, Did ye never read in the scriptures, The stone which the builders rejected, the same is become the head of the corner: this is the Lord's doing, and it is marvelous in our eyes? (Matthew 21:42)*

I got the request to speak the day before the engagement and decided to spend the entire night before fasting and praying in preparation of what God would have me teach. I went to a place called the Glory Room. It was not very special. It was just a room up high in a church without chairs of couches, just a floor, walls and lights. It was open all the time for prayer. Many nights it is full of all kinds of saints praying. This night it was empty. I fasted, prayed and studied all night. Up in that room I asked God for a word to teach and for signs and wonders that would endorse the word as truth to those that listened. God gave me a word I still remember it until this day. It was taken from Act 1, John 13, and Act 2. Then God gave me a vision. I saw the service that was to take place the following morning. I did not see my self teaching, instead, I saw the audience that would attend. It was the same view I had the next day when I began to teach. That night I could tell you where people would sit. Not just the students, but the visitors that always like to sit in on the classes of the ministry school. In the vision I even knew the colors of the clothes they would wear. For some reason, those colors seem important in the vision. Then God began to identify what miracles he would perform and to whom. He showed me in a vision the people I would lay hands on and pray. He told me their needs I would use to confirm and to assure them God was going to miraculously answering their prayers. I saw all of this in a vision the night before.

So when I walk in to teach, I could hardly contain myself. It was like I was once again lifted up by two people, one on my left and one on my right. I could hardly get the words out my mouth while I taught, because I knew what God was about to do. And he did it. I finished teaching and asked everyone to stand and pray. After I led the audience in prayer, I began to reveal the needs of the saints and call them to the front. I did not know their names, but I knew their needs. I also knew there faces from the vision the night before and strangely, I remembered what color clothing they would be wearing. So I would call them to the front by telling them what color clothing they were wearing while my eyes were closed. It was very strange. I said, "The man with the brown shirt that is wearing a tie on my left please come forward, God has a blessing for you. You know who you are, because God has put in your heart you are the person." I then walked to the other side of the church and said, "The young lady in the blue skirt and white blouse, God wants to give you the answer to your prayer for a healing, come forward and receive it. Yes, don't look around, it is you." When I called them, I never open my eyes to look up, since I was calling people based on my vision and not based on whom I saw sitting in the audience. Most of the time, my eyes were closed or I was only looking down as I walked from one side of the church to the other just to make sure I did not trip (over people that began to gather at the alter as I called them). When they came forward, I would lay hands on them and tell them about the need God had shown me in the vision, pray for them, and then thank God for the answer to the prayer. Most were slain in the spirit by Jesus when I touch them (and that is why I had to look down to walk from one side of the church to the other). This signs and wonders portion of the class was a total surprise to everyone, for I had told no one of the vision I had from Jesus. So there were about 10 people on the floor slain in the spirit before someone realized some men ought to take the responsibility to be catchers of saints slain in the spirit. A sister friend in the Lord commented later that day, God was really doing a work, because no one was hurt when they went down without catchers. She said, "Some went down very hard making a very loud noise". I did not notice at the time, because I was very much caught up in the spirit. God was working on me that day as much as he was working on the receivers of the blessings. The fact I never lost my place was also very shocking to me. At any given time I was calling five to six people forward. They came forward in different orders from the order in which I called them. When I stopped calling to pray for one, I had no problems in knowing the specific needs of the person standing in front of me. Even when the order was mixed up and the number of people lying all over the floor had become so many I could no longer tell from where in the audience the person in front of me for pray came. I somehow knew the need anyway the second I touched the person.

I remember saying, "an elderly couple on my left has been in pray for some time for a miracle from God and has not received it." I stated, "You will know I am talking about you, just look at each other and you will know". I asked them to come forward and went to pray for others that had already come forward. Later that same day, a close friend in Christ that was a bible student in that class said he watch every couple on my left and noticed only one couple looked at each other after I made the call for them to come forward. When they looked at each other, they both started crying and came forward. None of the other couples on my left looked at each other or moved from their seats. There were many couples on my left, but only one heard from God. That couple got their miracle that morning. This was a mighty blessed day in the Lord. For about 30 minutes, God was really pouring out his Living Water. When it ended or rather when my time slot for teaching had come to an end, I was still very much caught up in the spirit. A very dear sister in Christ came forward and thank God in my presence she had decided to attend class that morning. She then put her hands on my head and said, "Receive rest in the Lord". I was slain in the spirit and that is how the Lord brought me back to the natural world. This same very dear sister in Christ turned out to be very important in the required qualification of my ministry for ordination many months after I taught the class.

I know many are thinking it all just smoke and murals. It was just a lot of emotions caught up in the moment. Well maybe you think you are right. But you are the judge if you refuse to trust the truth in faith. I only ask you do the investigation first. You see, the entire class was recorded on voice tape. Obtain and listen to the recording first and then decide if it was or was not of God. As for me I know.

I Am Come To Bring Living Water

Therefore we ought to give the more earnest heed to the things which we have heard, lest at any time we should let them slip. For if the word spoken by angels was stedfast, and every transgression and disobedience received a just recompence of reward; How shall we escape, if we neglect so great salvation; which at the first began to be spoken by the Lord, and was confirmed unto us by them that heard him; God also bearing them witness, both with signs and wonders, and with divers miracles, and gifts of the Holy Ghost, according to his own will? (Hebrews 2:1-4)

Well after that once, I assumed it would not happen again. I mean, once was enough to give me the faith to trust God as never before, but it happened again.

Now do not become overly concern at my mentioning slain in the spirit. I know there are several ministers that believe this reaction of believers not to be one hundred percent of God. There basis of such a statement is they are not able to find the practice among the early believers in the bible. Well, I disagree. They are just looking under the wrong name for the experience. The use of the word "slain" is the only portion of this occurrence that is new. Try looking up in your bible the number of times someone would "fall down" in the presence of God, Jesus, or even the power of the Holy Spirit. It happened frequently in the presence of Christ. Even demons responded that way in Christ's presence. It happened to Paul when Jesus spoke to him. And if you research the Old Testament, you will also find time and time again, men falling to the ground in the presence of God. Within the body of Christ, we would be far better to search out the things that edify one another in the church rather than the things that divide one another (and the body of Christ).

I use to be a street minister in Florida. I worked on street corners outside of bars in Sarasota, Palmetto, and Bradenton Beach. The work was performed late at night while the bars were in high gear. I generally carried a group of ministry students each Friday and Saturday night with me right after evening church services. We arrived at about 11 PM and remain on the streets until the bars closed at about 3 AM. The ministry was very successful and many souls came to Christ. Some even went into the ministry. As expected this cause a little concern at the bars. They perceived us as a group of people preventing customers from coming into the bars. In reality, as they soon found, we remain in obedience of the local laws and soon became known as an aid to the police. The nights we were on the corners, were nights without law breaking incidences. In fact, the police would often bring people to us, rather than take them to jail for minor offenses. As a result, the local newspaper wrote an article about the street ministry. After reading the article, a chapter of the Full Gospel Business Men's Fellowship in a southern city of Florida invited me to be the speaker at one of their monthly breakfasts.

I think they wanted to hear testimonies of my experiences on the streets. I am not much for giving testimonies of myself to win souls for Christ, so instead I prepared a brief teaching message Thursday night before the meeting from the Word of God. I did not have time to go to the Glory Room the night before. The night before the speaking engagement was Friday night and I was on the streets every Friday and Saturday night. Once I finished the Friday night street ministry the night before the speaking engagement, a small group of the students helping me with the street ministry got in the car with me and began the long drive to the Saturday morning Full Gospel Business Men's Fellowship meeting. On the way, I had nothing to do since one of the students offered to drive us in my car. Everyone else in the car other than the driver and I were sleeping. So I prayed. I prayed for hours about the upcoming meeting. Once again, God showed me a vision of the meeting. I could see various people in the audience in the vision. I once again was told the needs of those people in the vision. I noted in the vision what color cloths people would be wearing. I was again caught up in the Holy Spirit.

When we arrived, I knew what must be done. We went in and I could hardly wait for them to complete the breakfast and let me start ministering. Using the words one man told me at the end of the service, "When you started teaching the scripture, I just assumed this would be one more dull Saturday morning meeting, but by the end of the meeting this turned out to be the greatest spiritual meeting I have every attended in my life!"

I Am Come To Bring Living Water

God filled that room with his spirit and as I began to call people forward and tell them God told me there needs and was going
to answer those needs, few of us could retain our joy. God
healed the sick of many illnesses, delivered some from the desire
to sin, renewed love in the hearts of men that wanted to leave
their families, touched souls that hungered for his presence, and
gave love, joy, peace, longsuffering, gentleness, goodness, faith,
meekness, and temperance to many that morning. God was en-
dorsing his Word with miracles right before our eyes. Those that
were traveling with me were just as amazed as I. I called men
forward, told them what God had told me, lay hands on them
prayed and God slain them in the spirit and granted their needs.
Yes, those full grown masculine men were being slain in the
spirit by God in front of all their macho friends. God was showing his mighty power that morning. And God was showing me
his calling for my life. But, I was not ready to understand and
answer the call. God was using signs and wonders to endorse his
Word.

Maybe the true importance of the Full Gospel Business
Men's Fellowship breakfast meeting is not fully understood.
This is a meeting of men. Women were not in attendance. If you
walk into any Christian church, you generally will find many
more women than men. I do not know why. Maybe men are just
not interested in salvation. I also find women are usually more
excited in the church and seem more subjective to the Holy Spirit
than men. I know within the body of Christ there is truly no difference between men and women, but here on earth and in the
world that is not true. So when I go to a meeting of men and
nothing but men and God does an outpouring of his Spirit with
signs and wonders, I know deep down inside I serve a mighty
God. A God that is more than able to break the hard stubborn
back of a masculine proud man and make him become as a child,
cry like a baby, bow down and postulate hobble before God his
Savior. That is the true importance of that morning. It was not
the healings, the blessing, or the fulfillment of the vision I saw,
but the miracle of the breaking down of the strong houses of
those grown men. It was the change God made in their lives. It
was the change God made in the hearts of all those that witness

those signs and wonders that morning even if they did not personally receive a blessing. And it was all the souls that were not at the meeting, but heard about the mighty outpouring of God that morning and believed God is real just from the hearing.

> *No man can enter into a strong man's house, and spoil his goods, except he will first bind the strong man; and then he will spoil his house. (Mark 3:27)*

Signs and wonders are something that seems to have been loss over the years since Christ resurrection, but signs and wonders are something the time has come to find again. For the second time, God was showing me how signs and wonders come with Living Water, the Spirit of God. Yes, I did relate signs and wonders with Living Water for they are related. The signs and wonders endorse the calling of the Lord on my ministry. It is how you may know I am come to bring Living Water.

> *God also bearing them witness, both with signs and wonders, and with divers miracles, and gifts of the Holy Ghost, according to his own will? (Hebrews 2:4)*

Prophesy Of Living Water

Living Water is mentioned four times in the New Testament (John 4:10, John 4:11, John 7:38, and Revelations 7:17). In the Old Testament, it is found four times (Songs of Solomon 4:15, Jeremiah 2:13, Jeremiah 17:13, Zechariah 14:8).

In the Old Testament, Living Water is presented first as an opportunity for joy. The book of Songs of Solomon is love story illustrating the love between Christ the King and his lover and bride to be, the church (his body of believers). What better way to explain the love we have for Christ than to pattern it after a love affair between a King (Solomon playing the role of the Prince of Peace) and his bride (the saints making up the church Christ shall redeem and unite unto himself as one)? An image of Christ showing his love for his church by describing his lover's character is portrayed in the mist of this great symbolic love affair. He begins by speaking of a journey he makes with his love from Lebanon as his bride, traveling from Amana (near Damascus - a place infested with the devouring lion and swift leopard) to Shenir. This is symbolic of the Church leaving its place known as home where it is accepted by the world because in reality it is a place of great danger.

> *My soul is among lions: and I lie even among them that are set on fire, even the sons of men, whose teeth are spears and arrows, and their tongue a sharp sword. (Psalm 57:4)*

Christ speaks of his church as having charmed him with just a single glance and a single strain from the necklace. Christ is delighting in the affection we saints (the church) have for him. He speaks of the fragrance of the perfume of the Church (meaning the gifts, the fruits, and the obedience of the Church). He speaks of the lips of the Church being drip in honey and of honey and milk being under the tongues of the Church. It is the words of praise coming from our lips and our tongues every speaking the things of Christ.

Let the words of my mouth, and the meditation of my heart, be acceptable in thy sight, O LORD, my strength, and my redeemer. (Psalm 19:14)

Christ speaks of his Church as being a garden that is locked and a spring that is sealed meaning the Church is sealed from the world. The Church is call out of the world and locked away from the world by a born again experience that started a new life washing away the sins of the world. The new life is sealed by the spring of water, the Holy Spirit. That new life is a paradise that produces pomegranates and the best fruits, flowers and nard. Our new life in Christ bears fruit. It is not just a witness to others to bring them into the Church, but it is the love, joy, peace, gentleness, and longsuffering spiritual fruit of the saints.

But the fruit of the Spirit is love, joy, peace, longsuffering, gentleness, goodness, faith, Meekness, temperance: gainst such there is no law. (Galatians 5:22-23)

Then Christ says the Church is

A fountain of gardens, a well of living waters, and streams from Lebanon. (Song of Songs 4:15)

Christ says we are the fountain meaning the spring in the garden. And that spring is a spring of Living Waters.

The early Jews had practices concerning running water. They were required to assure waters they touch were alive so they would not defile there bodies. Living Water was water that was running so it could not become stagnant. These Jewish practices were expansions of laws given by Moses related to the cleansing of sins and some afflictions affecting the Children of Israel.

And when he that hath an issue is cleansed of his issue; then he shall number to himself seven days for his cleansing, and

I Am Come To Bring Living Water

wash his clothes, and bathe his flesh in running water, and shall be clean. (Leviticus 15:13)

But the Living Water Christ used here to describe his Church is not just running water, it is Living Water and this water flows from Lebanon (meaning God in Heaven). So the true Church of Christ has Living Water that flow from God by the vessel of his Son Jesus to his saints. What is this Living Water? Do we have this Living Water in the Church today? Or have we somehow drifted away from gift Christ gave us? Have we failed to receive what is ours or have we forgotten what we process? Have we forsaken his Living Water?

I use to teach the bible in several state prisons of Florida. I taught at the prisons for men in Ocala and Daytona. I had a great friend in the Lord and his wife that traveled with me. In fact my friend and I were ordained into the minister by our church at the same time. I also visited several other prisons for special services from time to time with other ministries. It was on one such visit I fully understood Christian life without Living Water (the Holy Spirit of God). I was participating in a prison revival being led by a minister out of Tampa. This visit actually took place before I started my teaching ministry in state prisons. In fact it was part of God's plan that led me into the prison ministry. The revival took place in two prisons. One was the men's prison in which I would later become a regular bible teacher with my friend in the Lord. The other was located across the road. It was one of Florida's two prisons for women. It was the first and only prison for women I have every visited to minister.

The format of this revival was to enter the prison have a testimonial service in the prison for men in the morning. Then the revival team formed two groups. One remain in the prison for men to eat lunch and fellowship with the men in a one on one format and the other went to the prison for women to eat lunch and have the same type of one on one fellowship in the prison for women. Then both team join forces for an afternoon testimonial service at the prison for women. The day ended with a social gathering with teams at each prison for more one on one counseling and fellowship.

I Am Come To Bring Living Water

I was assigned to the group that went to the prison for women because I was on program in the testimonial service. I was not a key speaker on the program. In fact my primary role was to be a one on one counselor for the entire revival. However, I had been asked to be on the program in the prison for women testimonial service to lead a prayer.

At the morning service in the prison for men and at lunch in the prison for women, I mostly listened. It was my first time working with this ministry and I needed to learn. I talked with several women while we were at lunch, but my fellowship with them was limited to those at the same table as myself. I had been instructed to not touch anyone while in the prison for women. There was great fear on the part of the guards that the men in attendance were the subject of potential sexual attacks from the women inmates. So there were several guards with us and close by at all times. A similar practice, I discovered later, was used in the prison for men for the women on the revival team.

As in the past and as is my practice when I know in advance I am to minister somewhere for the Lord, I prayed for several hours. And as in the past, God showed me a vision of the women's prison revival testimonial service. It was not a vision identifying specific needs and specific individuals. In stead it was a vision of dryness. It was a vision of people lacking a fulfillment. It was a vision of people reaching out to God as if they were in a dry desert dying for water. It was a vision of people dying from the lack of the spirit of God. I did not understand it at first, because I was under the impression the revival was bringing the spiritual water and the Word that was so needed. But after witnessing the morning meeting in the prison for men, I knew it truly was a testimonial service with various speakers giving personal testimony of how they came to believe in Jesus. The service lacked the Word of God. The service lacked the Spirit of God. The service seemed to glorify man more than Jesus. The service had forsaken the Living Water.

The hand of the LORD was upon me, and carried me out in the spirit of the LORD, and set me down in the midst of the valley which was full of bones, And caused me to pass by

28

I Am Come To Bring Living Water

them round about: and, behold, there were very many in the
open valley; and, lo, they were very dry. (Ezekiel 37:1-2)

God showed me in a vision how he would pour out his Spirit on the women attending the testimonial service. He told me what to do when I prayed. My excitement level was not as high this time as it had been when I previously had a vision about my ministry. In fact, I had a lot of fear because it was a prison and I was not the minister responsible for the revival. But to do what the Holy Spirit directs is always my one task in life.

The testimonial service was in the rear of the prison out on a baseball field. The entire revival team was on the audience side seated in the bleachers. A small podium stage was erected behind home plate. All of the women inmates were out on the baseball field. They were required to stand for the entire service. The guards were stationed around the perimeter of both groups. In between the revival team and the women prisoners was a chain link fence. It was 10 feet high around home plate and four feet high for the rest of the area in front of the bleachers.

The guards got all the women inmates on the field first while the revival team waited inside a locked room. Then they escorted the revival team to the field as one collective group surrounded by several guards. I still remember the amazement in my heart when I saw the chain link fence that was in my vision.

When the time for me to pray came and I was introduced, I went to the podium and stood with my head down for about half a minute. I was praying God would be with me as I did what he requested. I prayed the guards would understand.

I lifted up my head unto the hill from whence come my help and said, "God is going to pour his spirit out in this place upon each and every woman here that desires to receive a touch from God. This is not going to be a healing, but a sign. It will be a miracle. It will be a touch from the finger of God in this place. I cannot touch anyone here. Those are the rules given to me. God is not bound by those rules and he can touch anyone here even behind these prison walls. Come forward and touch this fence in front of you. If you cannot get to the fence, then touch the woman in front of you that is touching the fence. When I pray,

29

I Am Come To Bring Living Water

God almighty is going to extend his finger from Heaven to earth and touch this fence. Anyone connected to this fence will feel the touch of God in their life. They will be instantly changed, renewed in spirit, filled with his Holy Spirit and praise. Afterwards, the power of God's touch will remain in all that touch this fence and be manifest in love, joy, peace, gentleness, longsuffering, and temperance. You will be filled with all you need to survive being in this prison."

The women came forward, touched the fence, and I prayed. God touch that fence and all at once no one could hold onto the fence. As if electricity was sparked into the fence, all at once all the women let go and were pushed backwards away from the fence. Some fell backwards slain in the spirit, some fell to their knees in praise, some leaped and jumped for joy, and other ran wildly around on the baseball field. The entire revival team rose to their feet in total shock of what they were witnessing. In my mind, I was thinking, now that is a testimony of the Lord. Nobody but the Lord did this. Nobody on this revival team touched a single inmate. But look what the touch of the finger of God has done. My prayer was short, but the impact took thirty minutes away from the service as the leaders tried to recover what they called order.

As a result, Living Water had been poured out in that state prison. Many who were hungry for the spirit of God were filled that day. That was all they needed, because with that one drink, they will never thirst again. Those that had forsaken the Living Water were now able to come back to that water.

Needless to say, I was immediately escorted out of the prison by three guards. There words were simple; "Do not ever do that again in a state prison". I am no longer welcome in that prison. I did not fully understand exactly what I had done so wrong. The Minister responsible for the revival explained it to me. He said, "You are not allowed to pray in a state prison in the minor you prayed". He said, "The guards know the apostles were able to pray and have angels open prison doors. When they saw you pray and the affect it had on women at the baseball field, they feared you would pray, open the prison doors, and allow all the inmates to escape. The guards believe the bible."

I Am Come To Bring Living Water

Then the high priest rose up, and all they that were with him, (which is the sect of the Sadducees,) and were filled with indignation, And laid their hands on the apostles, and put them in the common prison. But the angel of the Lord by night opened the prison doors, and brought them forth, and said, Go, stand and speak in the temple to the people all the words of this life. And when they heard that, they entered into the temple early in the morning, and taught. But the high priest came, and they that were with him, and called the council together, and all the senate of the children of Israel, and sent to the prison to have them brought. But when the officers came, and found them not in the prison, they returned, and told, Saying, The prison truly found we shut with all safety, and the keepers standing without before the doors: but when we had opened, we found no man within. Now when the high priest and the captain of the temple and the chief priests heard these things, they doubted of them whereunto this would grow. Then came one and told them, saying, Behold, the men whom ye put in prison are standing in the temple, and teaching the people. (Acts 5:17-25)

The saints of God that were with me conducting a revival in a prison had decided to forsake, meaning forget or ignore the Living Water. These saints decided to forget about the Holy Spirit just because the guards in the prison were afraid of what the Holy Spirit might do in the prison. This was the most significant example of quenching the Holy Spirit I have ever witness. Just think, not allowing the Holy Spirit to have his way because the guards of the prison (people in the world) were afraid. Not allowing the Holy Spirit to deliver the Word and power of God. Not allowing those that are seeking the Spirit of God to be filled. Not allowing them to drink of the Living Water of Christ. They had a few brothers and sisters talk about their own lives instead of having someone deliver the Word from God. What has every happened in a life or in their life that exceeds the outpouring of the Holy Ghost? What in my life exceeds the power of the Word of God? What kind of program could I ever plan to exceed the greatness of God's program led by the Holy Spirit?

Yet over and over again in the church and our lives today, we sometimes put our program and agenda before that of the Lord. What I witnessed in that prison was not so unique. I see it daily in the lives of so many Christians. When you lean to your own understanding, and fail to trust in God, you are putting your program before God's.

> *Trust in the LORD with all thine heart; and lean not unto thine own understanding. In all thy ways acknowledge him, and he shall direct thy paths. (Proverbs 3:5-6)*

Following the leading of the Holy Spirit requires having the faith to do what you do not understand. When you start to understand it, then you usually are not following the Holy Spirit. His ways are not my ways.

> *For my thoughts are not your thoughts, neither are your ways my ways, saith the LORD. For as the heavens are higher than the earth, so are my ways higher than your ways, and my thoughts than your thoughts. (Isaiah 55:8-9)*

Following the lead of the Holy Spirit requires performance on faith. It requires performance based on what you cannot see, feel, touch, smell, or taste. If I can grasp it naturally with my senses, then it is not of the invisible God who is beyond my senses.

> *Now faith is the substance of things hoped for, the evidence of things not seen. For by it the elders obtained a good report. Through faith we understand that the worlds were framed by the word of God, so that things which are seen were not made of things which do appear. (Hebrews 11:1-3)*

I almost decided that day prison ministry was not for me, it seem to quince the Spirit of God within me. Thanks are to God, I understood it was not the ministry that error but they that ministered that error. To that end, many were bless for many years as

I Am Come To Bring Living Water

God use my brother, his wife, and me in a mighty prison teaching ministry following that day.

What happened to those women at that fence was what the Holy Spirit wanted to happen. It was the result of following the guidance of the Holy Spirit. It was letting the Living Water flow naturally from Christ into me and out of my belly via my mouth and tongue to those women holding on to that fence. It was the touch of the finger of God. And no prison or prison guard is strong enough to stop the finger of God. I could not forsake the Living Water of God.

Jeremiah spoke of forsaken the Living Water. Twice he prophesied a time when the Jews would turn from the Living Water, a time when the Jews would forget the leading of the Holy Spirit of God. Jeremiah said the Lord pleaded with the children of Israel and wondered if they had changed Gods because they decided to do that which had no profit.

> *Wherefore I will yet plead with you, saith the LORD, and with your children's children will I plead. For pass over the isles of Chittim, and see; and send unto Kedar, and consider diligently, and see if there be such a thing. Hath a nation changed their gods, which are yet no gods? but my people have changed their glory for that which doth not profit. Be astonished, O ye heavens, at this, and be horribly afraid, be ye very desolate, saith the LORD. For my people have committed two evils; they have forsaken me the fountain of living waters, and hewed them out cisterns, broken cisterns, that can hold no water. (Jeremiah 2:9-13)*

The children of Israel forsake the Living Waters and instead used broken cisterns that can hold no water.

Christians are still experiencing the forsaking of the Living Water. They have the Living Water, but chose not follow the led of that water. They decide not let the Holy Spirit have his way. Just as those leading the revival in the prison chose to quince the spirit. Instead of following the leading of the Holy Spirit, they put on their own program because it is more acceptable to the world around them.

I Am Come To Bring Living Water

Jeremiah prophesied once Israel had forsaken Living Water, then they forsook their reward in the Kingdom of God. They risk having their names written in the earth. That means having their names taken from the lamb's book of life and eternally written in the book of all that will receive eternal damnation.

O LORD, the hope of Israel, all that forsake thee shall be ashamed, and they that depart from me shall be written in the earth, because they have forsaken the LORD, the fountain of living waters. (Jeremiah 17:13)

So it was prophesied, Christian are giving the Living Water at rebirth. They become the Living Water (the Spirit of God) as they ascend to the heavenly father. But some of the Christians will forsake the Living Water. They will become that which is not Christ. The pressures of the world will become too much to bear, and many will concede to forsake the Living Water, stop following the Holy Spirit, turn to the world's ways and loose their place in the lamb's book of life.

One other Old Testament prophet spoke of Living Waters. The prophet Zechariah spoke of yet another dispensation of Living Waters. Solomon spoke of the church being the Living Water, Jeremiah spoke of God's people forsaken the Living Water, but Zechariah spoke of the time when Jesus will return with a sword to conquer and rule this world. It is a time when Jesus will gather all the nations to Jerusalem to battle the world. Jesus will take the city of Jerusalem. Then Jesus will destroy all that have captured and tried to destroy Jerusalem (meaning all that have attempted to destroy the saints of God). He will go out from the city to battle the nations and with him will be the holy ones. In that day, there will be neither heat nor cold. There will be no difference between day and night for the light of Jesus shall turn the darkness into light and all things done in darkness shall come to light. And the Living Water, the holy people filled with the Spirit of God shall in that day go freely in and out of the city of Jerusalem (meaning in and out of the presence of God in Christ) and flow from sea to sea in winter and summer. They will cover earth from east to west and their Living Water shall never dry up in the heat nor freeze in the cold. Their Living Water will be ever flowing from one end of the earth to the other. The Kingdom of Heaven will be on earth and Christ will rule on the throne.

> *Behold, the day of the LORD cometh, and thy spoil shall be divided in the midst of thee. For I will gather all nations against Jerusalem to battle; and the city shall be taken, and the houses rifled, and the women ravished; and half of the city shall go forth into captivity, and the residue of the people shall not be cut off from the city. Then shall the LORD go forth, and fight against those nations, as when he fought in the day of battle. And his feet shall stand in that day upon the mount of Olives, which is before Jerusalem on the east, and the mount of Olives shall cleave in the midst thereof toward the east and toward the west, and there shall be a very great valley; and half of the mountain shall remove toward the north, and half of it toward the south. And ye shall flee to the valley of the mountains; for the valley of the mountains shall reach unto Azal: yea, ye shall flee, like as ye fled from before the earthquake in the days of Uzziah king of Judah: and the LORD my God shall come, and all the saints with thee. And it shall come to pass in that day, that the light shall not be clear, nor dark: But it shall be one day which shall be known to the LORD, not day, nor night: but it shall come to pass, that at evening time it shall be light. And it shall be in that day, that living waters shall go out from Jerusalem; half of them toward the former sea, and half of them toward the hinder sea: in summer and in winter shall it be. (Zechariah 14:1-8)*

Let me try to paint an image of what the prophet saw. You may find a picture provided in the canon bible scriptures is not clear, but if you study some of the lost scriptures (for example The Secret Gospel of John, The Origins of the World, The Revelation of Adam, and The Book of Thomas), you may begin to understand this image. Not that I proclaim the validity of any of the lost scriptures, but in my life I have learn to listen to God regardless of the vessel he uses to deliver his message.

Bring forth therefore fruits worthy of repentance, and begin not to say within yourselves, We have Abraham to our father: for I say unto you, That God is able of these stones to raise up children unto Abraham. (Luke 3:8)

In fact he is able to make a stone speak as easily as he made a burning bush speak to Moses. So I study the lost scripture as an aid to understand the canon bible.

God is a Spirit and we must worship him in Spirit and truth. God is invisible and incomprehensible. It is wrong to try to describe him with our language, for he is greater than any words in our languages. None of those words are capable of describing the character of God. But let me try to provide an inclination of what God is in my words. Image God as something that cannot be described in the center surrounded by its own glory. That glory is like a mirror that reflects an image of God which cannot be described who is in the center of the glory. The mirror is glory, pure light, pure reflection, or pure water. Another way to express it is pure Spirit. So when Jesus is seated at the right hand of God, he is in the midst of God's glory. He is in the midst of the pure light, pure reflection, or pure water. Jesus is therefore the pure Spirit that surrounds God. The glory of the father is the son. And the only way we can go home and be at rest with God is to be in Christ. We literally have to be born again and put on the body of Christ to be able to sit with Jesus at the right hand of the Father. Since nothing in the glory of God that surrounds God can be less than perfect, we must become perfect in Christ to one day enter into heaven and the rest of the Lord. We must accept and become the Living Water (the Spirit) of Christ to become part of the perfect reflection of God.

So I need this Living Water. No, I must have this Living Water. I must become the Living Water Solomon spoke of and not forsake the Living Water as Jeremiah prophesied, so I can become the Living Waters that flow in and out of Jerusalem that Zechariah spoke about.

The Promise Of Living Water

The first time Jesus described Living Water is found in the John 4. The chapter starts by revealing the fear of the Pharisees about the number of people being baptized by Jesus. But in reality, the scriptures do not record Jesus actually performing baptisms, but does indicate he may have baptized his twelve disciples. Perhaps he did. There are some that believe he baptized others and there are scriptures that indicate he may have, for instance at the time of his arrest, there was a man in his presence in the garden with only a linen cloth around his naked body. That was the required garment for the (all night lone) baptism historically known to be practiced by Jesus and his Disciples. Perhaps he was preparing to perform a baptism while he was in the garden that night.

And there followed him a certain young man, having a linen cloth cast about his naked body; and the young men laid hold on him: And he left the linen cloth, and fled from them naked. (Mark 14:51-52)

Regardless, the issue is the Pharisees assumed Jesus baptized many followers even if the actual baptism may have been performed by Disciples of Christ.

The fear of this practice by the Pharisees was based on their potential loss of money and power. Prior to the arrival of John the Baptist, the only way a Jew could be cleanse of any unclean act such as sin was to travel to the temple in Jerusalem and make an offering for his uncleanness. When the High Priest took two goats (one put to death and the other release to the wilderness), by which the uncleanness of the Jew would be taken away from him and the Children of Israel and placed in the wilderness.

And he shall take of the congregation of the children of Israel two kids of the goats for a sin offering, and one ram for a burnt offering. And Aaron shall offer his bullock of the sin offering, which is for himself, and make an atonement for him-

self, and for his house. And he shall take the two goats, and present them before the LORD at the door of the tabernacle of the congregation. And Aaron shall cast lots upon the two goats; one lot for the LORD, and the other lot for the scapegoat. And Aaron shall bring the goat upon which the LORD'S lot fell, and offer him for a sin offering. But the goat, on which the lot fell to be the scapegoat, shall be presented alive before the LORD, to make an atonement with him, and to let him go for a scapegoat into the wilderness. (Leviticus 16:5-10)

Now this was a very expensive effort on the part of the average Jew. The cost of traveling to Jerusalem and the time required was almost too much. Then once the Jew arrived, he had to buy the sacrifice animal. So this was time consuming and expensive for the average Jew. In addition the Pharisees had an opportunity to make a lot of money selling animals at the temple, not to say much about the power they process by being the only avenue for the forgiveness of the sins.

When John the Baptist started preaching and baptizing in the wilderness, it was a great savings to the people and it was an affront to the power of the Pharisees. You see, you can find water anywhere to perform a water baptism for the forgiveness of sin and the cleaning of the people. The cost of becoming cleansed from sin had just been greatly reduced. When Jesus continued the practice and baptized even more, the Pharisees decided something had to be done to stop this practice. So you understand the conflict arising between Jesus and the Pharisees. The Pharisees were being very clear about their dislike of the baptism practices of John and Jesus. So likewise, Jesus needed to show or teach the need for his baptism in the Holy Ghost.

Jesus really needed to clarify his baptism. He needed to show why his baptism should be preferred to the sacrifice of the High Priest.

When therefore the Lord knew how the Pharisees had heard that Jesus made and baptized more disciples than John, (Though Jesus himself baptized not, but his disciples,) He left

I Am Come To Bring Living Water

Judaea, and departed again into Galilee. And he must needs
go through Samaria. (John 4:1-4)

That clarification started when Jesus had to go through
Samaria to show why you and I must have a drink of Living Wa-
ter. Now it is true the road from Judaea to Galilee went through
Samaria, but it is not the only reason why Christ went through
Samaria. And it is also true Jesus gave his disciple an order not
to perch unto the Gentiles or go into the city of Samaria.

These twelve Jesus sent forth, and commanded them, saying,
Go not into the way of the Gentiles, and into any city of the
Samaritans enter ye not: (Matthew 10:5)

Note Jesus did not go into the city; instead he stopped at the
well near the city. His disciples went into the city to buy meat.
So Jesus did not violate his own instruction.

(For his disciples were gone away unto the city to buy meat.)
(John 4:8)

But verse four used strong wording, "must needs". The word
must (dei in Greek) means "it is necessary or it behoves". This
terminology is often used by Jesus when speaking of the work he
must perform for his Father. A word for word translation of the
fourth verse is "And it behoved him to pass through Samaria." It
means Jesus was led to go through Samaria by God, his Father.
The purpose was to teach a clarification of the baptism of Christ,
which is a baptism of Living Water.

Why did this message have to go to the Gentiles of Samaria
rather than to the Jews of Judea, Galilee, or even to the temple in
Jerusalem? This message had already been carried to Judea,
Galilee and even the temple in Jerusalem by the preaching of
John the Baptist. Remember the words of John the Baptist.

And I knew him not: but he that sent me to baptize with water,
the same said unto me, Upon whom thou shalt see the Spirit
descending, and remaining on him, the same is he which bap-

I Am Come To Bring Living Water

tizeth with the Holy Ghost. And I saw, and bear record that this is the Son of God. (John 1:33-34)

I indeed baptize you with water unto repentance: but he that cometh after me is mightier than I, whose shoes I am not worthy to bear: he shall baptize you with the Holy Ghost, and with fire: (Matthew 3:11)

So Jesus carried the message of a baptism in Living Water to the gentiles because the message had already been delivered to the Jews. The leaders of the Jews rejected the message of John the Baptist and sought to destroy him due to his threat on their profits in the Temple and their power over the people. The result of the rejected message is simply to take the message elsewhere that it may be heard and accepted. It is the approach Jesus taught in the parable of the marriage of the king's son.

The kingdom of heaven is like unto a certain king, which made a marriage for his son, And sent forth his servants to call them that were bidden to the wedding: and they would not come. Again, he sent forth other servants, saying, Tell them which are bidden, Behold, I have prepared my dinner: my oxen and my fatlings are killed, and all things are ready: come unto the marriage. But they made light of it, and went their ways, one to his farm, another to his merchandise: And the remnant took his servants, and entreated them spitefully, and slew them. But when the king heard thereof, he was wroth: and he sent forth his armies, and destroyed those murderers, and burned up their city. Then saith he to his servants, The wedding is ready, but they which were bidden were not worthy. Go ye therefore into the highways, and as many as ye shall find, bid to the marriage. So those servants went out into the highways, and gathered together all as many as they found, both bad and good: and the wedding was furnished with guests. (Matthew 22:2-10)

I Am Come To Bring Living Water

Had Christ tried to deliver this message to the Jews, the desire to destroy him may have come much sooner and prevented him from completing his Father's work.

When Jesus arrived at a parcel of land that Jacob had given to his son Joseph just outside of Samaria, he rested from his journey at Jacob's well. The journey he had made by foot with his disciples was about thirty-five miles. The area was a very dry land at the time Jesus ministered. In the summer months, the area was almost totally dependent on rain for clean drinking water. Often time, water was stored after rains. But even that water would not last long in the dry climax before turning undrinkable. There were a few underground fountains (springs or pools) that supplied water. Jacob's well was one such place feed by either an underground spring or pool. The well that is today said by many to be the same well is between 70 to 100 feet deep beneath limestone deposits.

Deciding to rest at that place was not an accident. The wells were very popular gathering places. Because the work of carrying water was assigned to women and often young women, the wells became a popular gathering place for young men seeking a wife. That is how Abraham found a wife for his son Isaac.

And the servant took ten camels of the camels of his master, and departed; for all the goods of his master were in his hand: and he arose, and went to Mesopotamia, unto the city of Nahor. And he made his camels to kneel down without the city by a well of water at the time of the evening, even the time that women go out to draw water. And he said, O LORD God of my master Abraham, I pray thee, send me good speed this day, and shew kindness unto my master Abraham. Behold, I stand here by the well of water; and the daughters of the men of the city come out to draw water: And let it come to pass, that the damsel to whom I shall say, Let down thy pitcher, I pray thee, that I may drink; and she shall say, Drink, and I will give thy camels drink also: let the same be she that thou hast appointed for thy servant Isaac; and thereby shall I know that thou hast shewed kindness unto my master. (Genesis 24:10-14)

I Am Come To Bring Living Water

Unfortunately, the well was also a popular gathering place for men and women seeking relationships outside of marriage. Where there is good, evil is always present. It is a law that will never change.

I find then a law, that, when I would do good, evil is present with me. (Romans 7:21)

Such was the case when Christ rested at the well.

There cometh a woman of Samaria to draw water: Jesus saith unto her, Give me to drink. (For his disciples were gone away unto the city to buy meat.) (John 4:7-8)

Jesus arrived at this well just in time to meet the woman of Samaria. She was very special. God had a unique calling for her. I know she was a woman of low essence in eyes of many saints. Maybe she even went to the well with the wrong intentions. She may have been looking for more than water. She may have been looking for a man. And here sat Jesus all along. His disciples were all gone into the city. This is the typical recipe for sin. A saint is all along in a strange place and confronted by an opportunity for evil. Who is to know? I have the desire. I have the opportunity. How can I resist this temptation?

Notice, the woman understood the opportunity she presented. She knew full and well Jewish men traveling from Judaea to Galilee generally traveled the shortest route through Samaria. She knew many would stop at Jacob's well to rest and refresh themselves. She knew she could tempt a Jewish man to sin. She knew no one would know, since Jews did not fellowship with Samarians. What Jew would ever ask a Samarian what happen? But just to make sure Jesus understood the opportunity for sin she reminded him.

Then saith the woman of Samaria unto him, How is it that thou, being a Jew, askest drink of me, which am a woman of

I Am Come To Bring Living Water

Samaria? for the Jews have no dealings with the Samaritans. (John 4:9)

With traps like this in the world, how do Christians keep themselves free from sin? The answer is to follow the example Jesus showed us while at the well. Jesus confronted the sin with the gift of God. I cannot fight battles with the desire to sin. I do not have the strength. But Christ within me is the armor, the sword, and the breastplate I need to put on to win this war. I let Christ fight the battles. I hide myself within Christ so sin will no longer see me, but instead see the Christ that is within me.

Jesus answered and said unto her, If thou knewest the gift of God, and who it is that saith to thee, Give me to drink; thou wouldest have asked of him, and he would have given thee living water. (John 4:10)

Jesus did not try to clarify why he was talking to a Samarian. To do so would have said he knew it to be wrong or unclean in the eyes of the law of the Pharisees. And once you start down the road of accepting the legal judgments of the Pharisees, it only leads to further acceptance. That is what the woman assumed Christ would do. But instead, he told her of the gift of God. Instead of going down the path of telling her what she assumed he was seeking (in her mind likely a sexual relationship outside of God and outside of the Jewish community hidden from Jews because it would be with a Samarian woman), he told her about a gift she was seeking. Jesus confronted sin with the gift of God. That gift was Living Water. That gift was the Holy Spirit. That gift was Christ. Jesus confronted sin with the greatest gift of all time, the love of God the father.

For God so loved the world, that he gave his only begotten Son, that whosoever believeth in him should not perish, but have everlasting life. (John 3:16)

Jesus said to the women, *"If thou knewest the gift of God."* Christ is that gift of God, but the women fail to recognize him.

I Am Come To Bring Living Water

Christ spoke as if the woman should have known he was the Christ. Again he said, *"and who it is that saith to thee, Give me to drink."* That is almost repeating the previous statement. Once again, Christ spoke as if the woman should have known he was the Christ and she should have because later she states the Samarians were expecting the Messiah.

Woman if you had recognized who I am (and she really knew in her heart) then you would have asked of me instead of me asking of you. Jesus said, *"thou wouldest have asked of him."* It is interesting he did not even identify what the women would have asked for, but that she would have asked. So it is with us Christians today, we do not always know what we want from the Lord, but in his presence, we know we want something from him. And that is alright, for once you have the Living Water, the Holy Spirit, it does not mater. We do not have to know what we need or want. The Holy Spirit will still make our request known unto God even when we do not know our request.

> *Likewise the Spirit also helpeth our infirmities: for we know not what we should pray for as we ought: but the Spirit itself maketh intercession for us with groanings which cannot be uttered. (Romans 8:26)*

Jesus said, *"thou wouldest have asked of him, and he would have given thee living water."* If this woman had known who she was talking to and what she really needed she would have cried out for Living Water, the Holy Spirit. Christ was offering to a Samarian that which was first made available and rejected by the Jews. John the Baptist said Christ would baptize with the Holy Ghost, but instead of Jewish leaders coming to Christ seeking the baptism, they rejected the baptism and Christ then offered it to the Gentiles.

Here is a very common, but often over looked truth in God's word. There is no respect of persons in the Kingdom of God.

> *For there is no respect of persons with God. (Romans 2:11)*

I Am Come To Bring Living Water

It is easy for us to accept God does not show any favoritism in his judgments, but we do not so readily accept the fact God also shows no favoritism in his blessings. I suppose we all want to think we are very special when it comes to being blessed by God. We are not. Yes we are his people and his blessings are upon those that hear and obey his Word, but of those that hear and obey, there is no respect of persons. God's answers to our prayers for blessings were performed or fulfilled long ago, even before we asked or were borne. Our willingness to accept those blessings is the only thing that is at issue. Saints of strong faith recognize their faith is based on the fact God has already done the work. He has already performed the miracle, the healing, or the provision of financial funds even before you made the request in prayer. All that is left is for you to accept the blessing and thank God.

The same is true with the opportunity for salvation and the baptism of the Holy Spirit. The work is done. Christ has already died on the cross, rose from the death, and sent us the Comforter. We only need to receive. If we are not willing to receive, then those blessings are available for whosoever will receive, for God is not a respecter of persons. He will bless the poorest, most ignorant person as easily as he will bless the richest, smartest person. In fact, it is easier for the poor to accept the blessings of God than it is for the rich. You see, the poor have nothing and will accept anything, while the rich have much and are more likely to compare the blessings of God to what they already have prior to accepting the blessings.

For it is easier for a camel to go through a needle's eye, than for a rich man to enter into the kingdom of God. (Luke 18:25)

So the gift of the Holy Spirit in the form of Living Water at the time of baptism was first offered to the Jews by John the Baptist. When the Jews refused the gift of God, Christ then offered this gift to the Gentiles.

I Am Come To Bring Living Water

Then said he unto him, A certain man made a great supper, and bade many: And sent his servant at supper time to say to them that were bidden, Come; for all things are now ready. And they all with one consent began to make excuse. The first said unto him, I have bought a piece of ground, and I must needs go and see it: I pray thee have me excused. And another said, I have bought five yoke of oxen, and I go to prove them: I pray thee have me excused. And another said, I have married a wife, and therefore I cannot come. So that servant came, and shewed his lord these things. Then the master of the house being angry said to his servant, Go out quickly into the streets and lanes of the city, and bring in hither the poor, and the maimed, and the halt, and the blind. And the servant said, Lord, it is done as thou hast commanded, and yet there is room. And the lord said unto the servant, Go out into the highways and hedges, and compel them to come in, that my house may be filled. For I say unto you, That none of those men which were bidden shall taste of my supper. (Luke 14:16-24)

The woman's response at the well was, who are you and what makes you so capable? Are you not talking about the very water in the well before you I have come here to seek? Where are you going to put it? You do not even have any of the tools used to draw the water. Her mind was set on things she could see, touch, smell, hear, and taste. These are the senses that operate in all our bodies. But these are senses of the flesh. They are not senses of the Kingdom of God. The Kingdom of God is spiritual and it may only be seen, touched, felt, smelled, or tasted spiritually. One positive sign that helps you know you are operating in the Kingdom of God is your natural senses no longer work. Faith deals with things I cannot see.

Now faith is the substance of things hoped for, the evidence of things not seen. For by it the elders obtained a good report. Through faith we understand that the worlds were framed by the word of God, so that things which are seen were not made of things which do appear. (Hebrews 11:1-3)

I Am Come To Bring Living Water

The woman was still looking at the physical world before her and asked if Jesus was greater than "our" father Jacob (denoting even as a Gentile Samarian, she is still a descendent of Jacob), who gave us the well and drank of it himself?

The woman saith unto him, Sir, thou hast nothing to draw with, and the well is deep: from whence then hast thou that living water? Art thou greater than our father Jacob, which gave us the well, and drank thereof himself, and his children, and his cattle? (John 4:11-12)

How many times do we face the greatest power that ever exist and ask if the power is greater than our petty problems? We actually ask God to heal our bodies, fix our families, grant us employment, feed us, and pay our bills as if these were the hardest task to perform on the face of the earth. In reality, when you think of the power and capability of God, then you realize our little problems are not that big to God. Consider two men of God preaching the Word. Both preach the Word of God in truth, but one tells of what miracles God can do and the other shows you a miracle of God. One is living in the flesh and only sees the physical world and the other is living in the spirit and knows the Spirit of God.

Jesus answered and said unto her, Whosoever drinketh of this water shall thirst again: But whosoever drinketh of the water that I shall give him shall never thirst; but the water that I shall give him shall be in him a well of water springing up into everlasting life. (John 4:13-14)

Hearing those words made the woman desire this water, even if she still visualized the water as natural water and not Living Water. Her desire was like so many of our prayers. They are amiss (evilly, grievously, or miserably) because we do not understand the Word of God and therefore do not know for what we should pray.

I Am Come To Bring Living Water

Ye ask, and receive not, because ye ask amiss, that ye may consume it upon your lusts. (James 4:3)

She wanted this water that when you drank, you never thirst again, but instead the water becomes a well within us springing up into everlasting life. That means water that once you drank; you will need no more for eternity.

The woman saith unto him, Sir, give me this water, that I thirst not, neither come hither to draw. (John 4:15)

The message of Christ is always simple and very plain. It does not require significant knowledge or even action on the part of the recipient to understand it. If it were not that simple, then why would so many turn from the world to Christ? But accepting Christ does bring new expectations for your life. After I was baptized as a child that was what my Grandmother tried to tell me. I did not really listen with any commitment at the time, but I do remember her telling me I was a new person in Christ. I was born again and some of the things I did prior to being born again, I am expected to no longer do. She gave examples like lying, stealing, cursing, and being disobedient. She tried to explain to me what being born again really meant in a way a child would understand.

That is the message Christ must now deliver to the woman at the well. She wanted this Living Water. She did not want to thirst anymore. She did not understand she had just asked Jesus to baptize her in the Holy Spirit. So Christ had to first teach her how to confess her sins and repent.

Jesus saith unto her, Go, call thy husband, and come hither. (John 4:16)

It only took a few simple words. Jesus did not lead her in a long sinner's prayer. He did not make a call for discipleship. He did not open the doors of a church for membership by baptism, letter, or Christian experience. He simply asked a question. But this was a question of conviction. Remember this woman may have been at the well looking for more than just water. She may have come to the well hoping to find a traveler, even a Jew that was looking for an out of marriage relationship in a strange country out of view of the Jewish community. Regardless of her intention, the words Jesus spoke convicted her heart and she confessed her sins.

In addition, the words of Jesus also pointed out to receive the Living Water, you need to be complete. In this case, you need join unto your husband and the two of you become one. Now the husband he refers to is not an earthly husband, but Jesus himself as the holy husband of the church. In reality, it should be our aims in life to one day become the bride that is joined to Christ in the bridal chambers where we become one body. That body being the body of Christ. Then we will be ready to stand before God and sit at his right within Christ. The Comforter can guide us the rest of our earthly life toward the goal of being one with Christ once we drink the Living Water (the Spirit of God).

The woman answered and said, I have no husband. Jesus said unto her, Thou hast well said, I have no husband: For thou hast had five husbands; and he whom thou now hast is not thy husband: in that saidst thou truly. (John 4:17-18)

God sees and know our sins. So when you are talking to God (meaning when you are praying), why brother to hide your sins. He already knows your sins. Would it not be better to openly confess those sins and request strength to overcome? Even if you do not have the will power to openly confess your sins in public; be truthful and open about the sins in your life at least in your closet talking to God. If you are truthful, perhaps Christ will use you as he is about to use this woman.

The woman now understood a little more about with whom she was speaking. She knew he was some kind of spiritual man, perhaps a prophet. How else could he know her life? How else could he know while she did not have a husband, she still had many men and even had one now that was not her husband. In today's world she would be called a prostitute or at lease a very promiscuous woman. With her sins in the open, she wanted to use the opportunity to understand a question that existed in Samaria. Samarians were not allowed to enter the temple in Jerusalem to worship God. So they established places in the mountains where they could worship God. So now was her opportunity to ask someone she perceived would know the correct place to worship God. Keep in mind she did not worship in the mountains. She did not worship at all. In fact, she may have been proclaiming to Jesus her lack of worship was the cause of her seeking so many men that would never become her husband or stay with her very long.

> *The woman saith unto him, Sir, I perceive that thou art a prophet. Our fathers worshipped in this mountain; and ye say, that in Jerusalem is the place where men ought to worship. (John 4:19-20)*

Note she never said she worshipped anywhere. Instead she posed a problem to Christ. My fathers went to the mountains to worship (and I think she knew this was wrong), but the Jew say we should go to Jerusalem to worship. Keep in mind; Gentiles were not welcomed into the temple in Jerusalem. So if Christ answered she should go to Jerusalem, then she would be justified in her lack of worship.

Why do some people try so hard to justify their actions, even when they know they are wrong? It is much more efficient and easier to acknowledge the wrong and then spend the time and effort correcting the wrong. You should not fear judgment. There is only one that may judge you. Even if a fellow saint points out your fault, they cannot judge you and remain obedient to God. So the only person that sees your wrong you should care about is God. Anybody else that sees the wrong does not matter. So why are you trying to justify your actions to God? You are not telling him anything he does not already know. Is it not better to say, "Lord, forgive me and help sin no more?"

I went to college at one of the Big Ten schools. I was just a little boy from Mississippi in a big northern college. Most people from Mississippi do not like to say it, but a high school graduate from Mississippi is a little bit behind an equivalent high school graduate from many northern states. Well I had to overcome that short fall, adjust to college life (away from parental guidance), and perform well.

When you look at the total of my college years, it seems I accomplished the task. I completed a four year degree in three and a half years. It sounds good for a little Mississippi boy. But that is not the whole story. You see I flunk out of college at the end of my first year for poor grades. The rules were simple, if you fail, you had to stay out of college for at least one semester, preferably one year and then you will be allowed to re-enroll and try again. Those were ok rules, but they overlooked the fact in my household, you never fail in school. It was just not accepted in my family. So I had to remain in school.

I went to the Dean of Freshmen. He was not talking to anyone. All students that failed were to talk to his assistants. His assistants had strict rules with no exceptions. If you talked to one of them, you were going home. So I got out of the line and looked for an empty room to go in and pray. I found the room, fell to my knees and began to pray. I heard a voice behind me, "Son can I help you?" I said yes, and followed the Dean of Freshmen into his office.

After small talk, he sent out for my folder. When he got it, he said, "Son, there is nothing I can do. I gave the direction to the others about no exceptions." Then all at once he got quiet, read a document in my folder and looked up with tears in his eyes. He said, "In all my years as a Dean, this is the first time I every saw a letter from a parent concerned about a student's unsatisfactory college grades." My mother had written the letter to the university and never told me about the letter.

The dean then told me about his son that die less than one month earlier. It was a suicide. He said, "I know my son was troubled. He also flunked out of college and I never cared enough to write his university. Now he is gone." The dean looked at me and said, I am not suppose to tell you this, but there is one way you can stay in school. He said you can ask the Business School to accept you as a student on probation, but you will have to almost make a straight "A" average for the next year. I said I would do it.

I Am Come To Bring Living Water

Great joy, it seemed settled. I still had to get the Business School to accept me. That was where I learned to stop justifying my wrong. The Dean of the Business School said he only had one question, what was so different about me now as opposed to the prior year that would justify a second chance. I started answering that question by telling him everything that went wrong the prior year. He said, "That is an unacceptable answer." I prayed and finally said, "I failed to be the student I should be. I made a big mistake my first year. I assumed I did not have to work to obtain my education." He looked at me and said, "If you really mean what you are saying, then you will make a straight "A" average and we will never have to meet again for the rest of your college years." Well I did make a straight "A" average for the next year and "A" average with only an occasional "B" average over the rest of my college career, but I never had to meet with the dean again and I finish the four year degree in three and a half years (and I failed one of those years). I learned it is better to confess your sin, ask for forgiveness and move forward. There is no way to justify sins.

Jesus saith unto her, Woman, believe me, the hour cometh, when ye shall neither in this mountain, nor yet at Jerusalem, worship the Father. Ye worship ye know not what: we know what we worship: for salvation is of the Jews. But the hour cometh, and now is, when the true worshippers shall worship the Father in spirit and in truth: for the Father seeketh such to worship him. God is a Spirit: and they that worship him must worship him in spirit and in truth. (John 4:21-24)

The Jews, God's chosen people, worshipped God in the Temple in Jerusalem. They assumed they worshipped correctly since they were obedient to the law left by Moses. But in many cases they were worshipping in ceremonies that praise the discipline of the ceremony and not the God that required the ceremony. The Samarians worshipped in the mountains. They were not sure who they worship. Some worshipped earthly Gods of stone or other material items. Others worshipped items of creation such as the moon and the stars. Neither group really understood what

---

or how to worship. In each case they were just following the practices of those that had gone before them.

The same takes place today. There are still many religions that worship the things God made rather than the maker of the things. These religions are not easy to recognize today. For instance, people do not line up to go in and bow before or praise and rejoice over a stone figure, but they do line up to go in and bow before, even praise and rejoice over a football team, a great singer, or a Hollywood star. In man's eyes these seem different, but what do you think they look like in the eyes of God? On a typical Sunday morning, there are a lot of people that go to some kind of church. Others at least will listen to a service on the TV or radio. But the number of people attending these functions is very small in comparison to the number of people that will tune in to the Supper Bowl game. If the church service starts getting too long, they are all upset, but they do not want the game to end. So many of us still do not know how and who to worship. We are just following the practices of those that have gone before us.

Jesus said the time is come when none of these methods of worship will be considered appropriate. There will be a time when you and I will not consider any of the aforementioned forms of worship as acceptable unto God. At that time we will finally understand God is a spirit and if you want to worship him, you have to worship him in spirit and truth.

Now the early Gnostic believers heard those words and said the key to worship was truth. In their minds that means true knowledge. So they created an entire belief system based on knowledge being the way to obtain eternal life. Meanwhile, the early church claimed them to be heretics. Well in most disputes there are some elements of truth and there are some elements of truth in this debate. The truth is very simple and it is knowing Christ is the son of God. It is not knowledge of man, but the knowing of Jesus that will save mankind. It is not your intellect knowledge that will get you to the reward of eternal life, but it is the knowing Jesus as your savior that will get you to eternal life. It would have been better if they had concentrated on worship in spirit more than on worship in truth.

I Am Come To Bring Living Water

That is what the woman at the well did. She knew the truth. She was already convinced the man she spoke with knew more than all those that went to the mountains and more than all men she had meant that went to the temple. She knew he was different. She was not sure who he was, but she knew he could see her whole life. Everything in this woman's life that was in darkness had just come to the light. This man knew all she had done in her life. That was the truth. It was the truth of her life. It was not some massive knowledge of the universe and creation. It was the simple truth she was a sinner living in sin.

It is just as simple for you and me. You do not have to know all the scriptures from Genesis to Revelations. You do not have to know how to work miracles or speak in tongues. You do not have to have twenty years of service in the church. You simply have to know you are a sinner. You simply have to be truthful about the sins in your life and that becomes the truth in your worship. Consider the two men on the cross beside Jesus. One said, *"save thyself and us."* The other rebuked him and said, *"we receive the due reward of out deeds."* He confessed his sins. He began to worship in truth and then said to the Savior, *"Lord remember me, when thou comest into thy kingdom."* And that is all it took for him to gain eternal life. He worshiped in truth. He knew this Christ. And he spoke words that could only be revealed spiritually. It does not take much. It is simple and it starts with the truth about self.

> *And one of the malefactors which were hanged railed on him, saying, If thou be Christ, save thyself and us. But the other answering rebuked him, saying, Dost not thou fear God, seeing thou art in the same condemnation? And we indeed justly; for we receive the due reward of our deeds: but this man hath done nothing amiss. And he said unto Jesus, Lord, remember me when thou comest into thy kingdom. And Jesus said unto him, Verily I say unto thee, To day shalt thou be with me in paradise. (Luke 23:39-43)*

God gave me a ministry of helping young people and I have work that ministry most of my life. It was not a ministry I sought out, but one that found me. I have worked with more than a hundred young people on a one-on-one basis. A large percentage of those actually lived in my home doing the time of the ministry. I have provided complete room, board, and care, legally adopted, temporarily housed, care in illness, comfort in dying, and visits in prisons and jails to many young people. I have had parents I did not even know existed drive over a thousand miles to bring a child to me and leave them to live with me without even asking me if it was ok. They just heard about me from a saint, prayed and followed God's guidance to bring me the child. These young people were in trouble. They were drug addicts, alcoholics, juvenile delinquents, satin worshippers, critically ill with terminal diseases, and just simply troubled young people. The problem may have been as simple as not being able to obey their parents or as complicated as being a drug dealer, or knowing they are going to die from illness in a matter of days. I have never understood why I was given this work; I just know I have performed it over the years.

One such young boy was only nine years old. He actually lived next door to where I was running a temporary shelter for transit people that were trying to become established in the community at the time. We became friends and often would just sit on the pouch and talk. We talked about what ever was on his mind. Then God reveal to us all, why he sent me this young boy. Doctors discovered he had a very bad heart. For the next year, he was in the hospital more than he was at home. You have to keep in mind; this was a young boy from a very poor family on welfare. They did not have the money to pay his medical bills. In fact, they did not even have enough money to pay to travel to the various out of town hospitals where he was usually transferred. I would often take off from my day job, to drive his mother across the state, so she could see her child. I tried as much as possible to comfort this young boy. He had great fear in those strange hospitals. He also had a fear of needles and the doctors in those strange hospitals seem to think he was a pin cushion. Many times while he was at home, he would ask his mother if he could come and spend the night at the shelter with me. For him, it was a chance to be away from the remainder of his family. They all seem to treat him as if he were already dead. He began to feel he had no worth.

The doctors finally decided what he needed was a heart transplant. The community went to work trying to secure the funding necessary to get this operation for a child on welfare. I initiated a state wide campaign to raise the funds. We raise a lot of money, but no where near what was required. Then God step in and convince a doctor on the other side of the country to perform the operation for free. The doctor's hospital also had an available and compatible heart. All that was left was getting the boy to the doctor. It took a lot of work, but God convince the Governor of the State to donate the use of his private plane to transport the boy.

So I took off again from my day job, traveled with the boy's mother to the hospital so she would be able to accompany her son on the trip. The night of the trip, I was talking to the young boy and God put it on my heart to make sure this young boy gave his heart to Jesus. It is interesting, with all that had transpired between us in past discussions, I had never asked him if he knew Jesus. I asked that night and found no one else had ever asked him that question. We prayed and he gave his failing heart to Jesus.

Latter that night, when they were ready to transport him to the plane, the ambulance drivers refuse to transport him to the airport without a payment. By the time we convince them otherwise, it was too late. The little boy had become unstable and never recovered. He went to the Lord that night. Just minutes from the plane and hours from the hospital with a new heart waiting for him, he gave up his life. I remember thanking Jesus I had time to introduce the boy to Christ.

This little boy did not have time to live a Christian life. He did not have time do a lot of good before he went home. He did not have time to memorize hundreds of bible verses. He did not even have time to join a local church of any denomination. All he had was his truthful confession of sin and his spiritual belief in Christ. He only had time to worship God in Spirit and truth once in his life. I know he is with Jesus. You do not know about the whereabouts of all that past over to be with the Lord, but with some you are just sure. I am sure and that was my statement at his funeral. I told his family and friends (hundreds of them) he gave his weak sick and incapable heart to Jesus and he could not wait for another earthly heart in a transplant, because Jesus had a new heart waiting for him and that heart will last an eternity. In that place, there will be no more hospitals, needles, or doctors. My friend is at peace at last in the rest of the Lord.

> *But the hour cometh, and now is, when the true worshippers shall worship the Father in spirit and in truth: for the Father seeketh such to worship him. God is a Spirit: and they that worship him must worship him in spirit and in truth. (John 4:23-24)*

If worshiping the Father in spirit and in truth requires us to be truthful about sin in our own life, then what is meant by the spirit part?

There are a lot of studies about the creation of the world and the creation of man. It is just one of those areas that over the years always attracted a lot of attention and study. I have studied many of these theories. By that I mean the Christian theories. There are several other theories outside the church. I have also study antiquity writing (the lost scriptures) on the subject. Without getting into all the debates about what is found in the cannon text on the subject as opposed to what is ascribed in other texts, there is some basic truth with which everyone agrees.

> *And the LORD God formed man of the dust of the ground, and breathed into his nostrils the breath of life; and man became a living soul. (Genesis 2:7)*

God breathed the breath of life into the nostrils of man and he became a living soul. Most Christian bible scholars will agree the portion of man that was not made from the material things of the earth is the portion man received directly from God, being the breath. This breath is the Hebrew word "neshama" and means wind, inspiration, blast, intellect, soul, or spirit. Essentially, God put his Spirit into man. Man has often ignored this Spirit within him, because it is contrary to the world around us. So we conform to the world's ways and fail to recognize the Spirit of God within us. It is as if the Spirit of God within us is in a deep sleep. There are many of the earlier antiquity writers of scriptures outside of the canon that really believe man is still asleep.

And the LORD God caused a deep sleep to fall upon Adam, and he slept: and he took one of his ribs, and closed up the flesh instead thereof; And the rib, which the LORD God had taken from man, made he a woman, and brought her unto the man. (Genesis 2:21-22)

They believe man never really awaken from the deep sleep that fell upon him. I do not know if they are right or wrong, but I do know God put his Spirit inside of us and for so many of us, the Spirit is inactive as if it were asleep. Some just say man is living in sin and does not hear God. They think of God as something outside of man coming into man and changing him. But I know when God knots on the door of the heart of a sinner; he is not knocking on the door of an empty house. There is someone or something at home. I believe it is the Spirit of God that is already inside of us. All that happens, when I come to Christ, is the awaking of that Spirit. Notice Christ never gave the woman at the well the Living Water, because she already had Living Waters. She just needed someone to awaken the stream of Living Water that was already inside her. That is my calling. I am come to bring Living Water. Not that I have any pots of water in some back room. No I am just called to awaken the Living Water that is already inside of you. I am called to awaken the Spirit of God inside of you.

Worshiping God in Spirit is finding this element of yourself and allowing that portion of God that is within you to lift up praises to God almighty. It is like letting God praise himself. How else could our praises be found worthy other than those that are in Christ, those that are the image of God, and those that are the perfect refection of God? So when God sees us giving him praise and worship, he sees his son Jesus and he sees his own

Spirit. God sees his own reflection offering him worship and praise.

To reach this level of praise requires our elimination of our self and all we think we know about how to praise God. Remember, his ways are far from our ways. So to really praise God in spirit, you need to put aside all you know within the flesh about praise. I like to just close my eyes, turning off my natural senses. I like to forget those watching, where I am, and the structure of the service I am in and just open my heart to God. My actions (whether I lift my hands, clap my hands, stomp my feet, open my mouth in praise, cry out loud, or just sit completely quiet and still) does not matter and I give them none of my concentration. My every being is tone to God and praise for him. Sometimes, I start by thanking him for what he has done for me. When I think of his goodness, his loving kindness, his blessings, his guidance, his word, his revelations, and the joy he has given me, I just explode with praise. The key is when you worship in spirit, you will lack understanding in your mind. When you worship in the spirit, you will lack awareness of your worshiping with your senses. You will not be able to taste, feel, smell, touch, or see the worship. If you are relying of those senses for your worship, then you are not worshiping in the spirit. If you are concern with what somebody is thinking when they see you, then you are not worshiping in spirit. If you are concerned about the world (what you are going to cook when you get home or where you are going after service), then you are not worshiping in spirit. When the woman touched the hem of Jesus' garment to be made whole, she did not worry about what someone would say about how she was dress, or what she was doing, or about how someone would think her to be a poor sinner. Instead she just did what the Spirit led her to do without any fleshly concern.

And, behold, a woman, which was diseased with an issue of blood twelve years, came behind him, and touched the hem of his garment: For she said within herself, If I may but touch his garment, I shall be whole. But Jesus turned him about, and when he saw her, he said, Daughter, be of good comfort;

I Am Come To Bring Living Water

thy faith hath made thee whole. And the woman was made whole from that hour. (Matthew 9:20-22)

That is the kind of faith required to worship God in spirit. You have to just believe that which makes no worldly sense. You have to believe your praise and worship is in the presence of God in the Kingdom of God. I know it makes no sense. But such is the Kingdom of God; it is not the world we know. In fact it is the opposite of the world we know. You are no longer in control. The control has shifted to part of you that God himself breathed into your body. The Spirit of God is in control. Your spirit has entered the holiest of holy and is before the presence of God. You body is just going along for the ride.

It does not make sense. It is not suppose to make sense. That is what faith is all about. Now have faith and trust God. Worship him in spirit and truth.

Did you know God wants it that way? The scripture says, *"the true worshippers shall worship the Father in spirit and in truth: for the Father seeketh such to worship him."* God is looking for worshippers that will worship him in spirit and truth. That is why he sent his son to save us. Jesus came to save us and retrieve the Spirit of God that is within us. He came to bring that spirit back to God so that spirit may worship God eternally. It is the completion of God. Not that God needs us to be complete, but that we need him to be complete. We are like a mirror without the image that appears in the mirror. We have need of reality to complete our image. So when it is complete, God will look out on the Living Water (the Spirit that surrounds God) and see him glorifying, praising, and worshiping himself. It is like you looking in the mirror every morning, you expect to see yourself. God expects to see himself in the Living Water, his Spirit and image of himself. God is seeking your spiritual worship so you may be completed in Christ and one with the Father, Son, and Holy Ghost.

By now you may think I am off the deep end. Maybe I am, but that is why I am right. If I agreed with what is in your mind, then I would disagree with that which is of God. If you do not understand, you are not along. Many will hear and will not believe or understand. It is very hard to accept this message. But blessings are upon them that hear it and believe. Greater blessing are upon them that have not heard, but already believe and curses are upon those that will not hear and greater cruses on those that hear and believe not.

The woman at the well heard the message. She believed the message and cried out of her spirit.

The woman saith unto him, I know that Messias cometh, which is called Christ: when he is come, he will tell us all things. (John 4:25)

Her spirit was awakening. She still did not know who this man was, but she at once began to proclaim her Savior was coming. It is so strange, the poor, the rejected, the sinners, the unlikeable of the world, the underdog, the stone the builders rejected, and the last person you would turn to for help often becomes the one God will use mightily to deliver us from the grip of the world. Here this woman that was in our terms today a prostitute, a whore, a woman of the night, an adulterer, and a woman of very low respect, is the one Christ raises up to be the first Gentile to come to the Father. And not only a sinner of low esteem, but he selects a woman instead of a man.

Here you must understand a principle of the Kingdom of God. It is the nature (meaning a structural law) of the Kingdom of God. You will find this principle true in every parable Jesus taught of the Kingdom of God. You will find this principle true for all time as you seek the Kingdom of God. There are several of these principles and if one can understand each, one can understand the Kingdom of God. I will discuss one of these principles, but that you may know all you desire to know, here are a few of these principles I will not include in this discussion.

o The last shall be first and the first shall be last in the Kingdom of God
o The beginning and the end are one in the same in the Kingdom of God

61

I Am Come To Bring Living Water

- The seeds you sow will result in saints greater in the Kingdom of God than you
- Your salvation will be assured not by your work, but the work of those that received seeds you sowed in the Kingdom of God
- The way of the Kingdom of God is the opposite of the way of the world

The principle I will discuss is:

- The least is the greatest and the greatest is the least in the Kingdom of God

This is a Kingdom principle that applied to the woman at the well.

For there is no respect of persons with God. (Romans 2:11)

God does not reserve his great works for special leaders or those of high places. God usually does not use the rich and the high and mighty, but often uses the poor and those of low respect to carry out his purposes. Remember Christ told the rich man if you desire to be perfect, take sell all you have, give to the poor, and follow me.

Jesus said unto him, If thou wilt be perfect, go and sell that thou hast, and give to the poor, and thou shalt have treasure in heaven: and come and follow me. (Matthew 19:21)

To be perfect, he had to change his status in life. I did not say you should not have those successes of life, I simple said, God uses those of lower estate in his Kingdom. Other examples include Jesus describing the Kingdom of God as like becoming a child, the Kingdom of God as like the wedding feast or the dinner that the servants went into the highway and invited whosoever will come, and in the selection of the disciples, Jesus did not select a single Jewish leader. In fact, Jesus was not a Jewish leader and yet he was the Son of God. He was of such a lowly estate in the church of his time he was not allowed to even see or enter into Holiest of Holy place in the Jewish Temple on earth, yet being the Son of God, he was the only Jew that was allowed to enter into the presence of the Father in the Kingdom of God. Sometimes, I think God decides to use those of low estate just to show the great power of God that exceeds any and everything the world is capable of accomplishing. It shows God is able to move mountains.

There are many more examples that prove this principle of the Kingdom of God. Here is a list of a few.

o David fighting Goliath
o David (the youngest son) anointed King instead of his older Brothers
o An ex-slave and ex-inmate name Joseph delivers the children of Israel from phantom
o The selection of a murderer named Moses to deliver the children of Israel from Egypt

So Jesus selected this woman at the well, offered her Living Water and reveals himself as the savior to her.

The woman saith unto him, I know that Messias cometh, which is called Christ: when he is come, he will tell us all things. Jesus saith unto her, I that speak unto thee am he. (John 4:25-26)

The woman's eyes are opening. Her sleeping spirit is awaking and seeking Christ. She remembers the promise of Christ coming and she remembers once Christ comes, he will tell us all things. She still does not know who she is talking with, but she believes the one she is speaking with knows about Christ and his coming, because he seems to know more than those that are worshiping in the mountain and those that are worshiping in the temple. Then Jesus makes it very clear and says, *"I that speak unto thee am he."*

Notice, the woman never questioned the claim of Jesus. It would be so wonderful if the world would accept Jesus this way.

I Am Come To Bring Living Water

The number one reason so many refuse to believe is they depend on their own intellect to determine if Christ is really the son of God. If you have ever tried to reason with an atheist, then you know no amount of reasoning will provide an acceptable argument that Christ is the son of God. They cannot rationally believe the son of God that made the world walked the face of the earth. So the atheist will begin to produce arguments that defy reasoning. You may know the usual list like:

o   How did God make heaven and earth in seven days?
o   How did Jonah live inside a fish?
o   How can the same person be the Father, Son, and Holy Ghost all at the same time?
o   Do you really believe it is possible for a virgin to have a child and remain a virgin?
o   How can one God hear every prayer prayed by every believer on the face of the earth and never miss a single one even when multiple people pray at the same time?
o   Why does God allow evil and why does he not just get rid of the devil?

And the discussion always seems to end with the believer saying, "You just have to accept these things on faith" and the atheist saying to the believer, "You are just refusing to be rational and use your mind. You know in your mind these things are not possible." Well the atheist is correct. We are not using our minds. What in my mind is capable of understanding God? The only reason I have got a mind is because he gave me one. God is a Spirit. My mind is not capable of being spiritual or even understanding things that are spiritual. I will not agree with the believer that says I have to just accept Christ on faith, I would prefer to say I have to accept Christ in Spirit because I do not know of any other way to accept him. Now I know accepting him in Spirit exercises my faith to believe, but while the atheist is not willing to believe based on faith, he may be willing to try to intellectually understand the Spirit of God. Such a venture on the part of the atheist may well result in a spiritual experience that will bring them to God. Let me provide a very simple example. I

64

cannot see, feel, touch, taste, or smell the Spirit. I have no senses that will tell me the Spirit exist. I also cannot accept the existence of the Spirit on faith, for even a Christian will tell you there is a substance or evidence (something real I can see, feel, touch, taste or smell) to faith. So how can I believe in the Spirit if I have no evidence or substance? Well, I cannot see, feel, touch, taste or smell the wind or air, but they are there and my body accepts they are there every time I take in a breath. If I stop breathing just because I cannot find the evidence or substance of the wind or air, I will stop living. Just as the air I inhale is real, so is the Spirit of God. If I never experience the faith to accept him, my body must acknowledge his Spirit exist or I cannot live anymore just like I cannot live without the air. If God does not exist, then:

o   Who or what keeps the sun from falling on my head?
o   Who or what cause the big bang I was taught in school to believe to happened?
o   Who or what started evolution?
o   And who controlled evolution to assure I evolved into a man rather than a cow?
o   If a man can make a submarine that will allow a man to stay alive under water for months at a time with his little mind, then why can not God who made man make a fish that keeps a man alive for a few days? The fish eats food and breaths in the water, so why can not the man do the same inside the fish? Maybe if man spent some time understanding how God's fish can take air out of water, we would not have to store air in our submarines to keep men alive. Maybe we could learn to take it from the water too.
o   If water can be in the form of liquid, ice, and steam, then why can not God be in the form of the Father, Son, and Holy Ghost?
o   If I can believe a man evolved from a one cell animal that was swimming around in the water that bears no resemblance to a man, then why is it so hard to believe a woman with a close womb that has known no man can have a baby? If I believed the one cell animal became impregnated by itself, pro-

duce something that was not like itself and still continued to live as a one cell animal afterwards we find in water swimming today then I can also believe in a virgin birth.

o I sit in front of a TV watching a football game and yell at the players believing and fully expecting them to respond and do what I say while I know a million other viewers are doing the same thing in front of their TVs, so why is it so hard to believe God can hear all of our prayers a once.

o Why does a child being watched by his parent and told to stop doing something wrong continue to do the wrong as if his parents cannot see them? When it happens, the parent does not just kill off the child to get rid of the wrong. So why do you expect God to just kill off evil to get rid of the devil?

o If God who made day and night and holds the sun in the sky by day says he made heaven and earth in six days, why should I not believe him, since he still controls the number of hours the sun stays in the sky every day?

God is a Spirit and you need to just accept him spiritually. That means accepting him beyond your understanding. You will never understand that which is spiritual. At least not until you become Spirit. One of best things to do when you go to church and worship God is to forget how you think. Just close your eyes, forget everything, lean not to any of your own understanding, lift your hands and praise God. You do not even need a signal or a time on the program outline by the pastor of when to start praising God. You just have to praise God. Believe me, God will create a time for your praise even if everyone else in the church stares at you and wonder what is wrong with you. That is the funny thing about being led of the Spirit; it will not make any sense. The Spirit will not be logical. The Spirit will not be outlined in any books of worship. The Spirit will not be of this world or of anything in this world.

That is what happened to the woman at the well. This little possible prostitute or promiscuous woman had her eyes opened and was filled with Living Water and caught up in the spirit. She no longer controlled her own actions. She lost all reasoning. She began to act unintelligent.

I Am Come To Bring Living Water

And upon this came his disciples, and marvelled that he talked with the woman: yet no man said, What seekest thou? or, Why talkest thou with her? The woman then left her waterpot, and went her way into the city, and saith to the men, Come, see a man, which told me all things that ever I did: is not this the Christ? Then they went out of the city, and came unto him. (John 4:27-30)

The disciples returned from town saw what was going on and wondered why is Christ talking to this Samarian? Why is he talking to this woman you could so easily assume came to the well looking for a man for sex? They wondered what she wanted from their master, and why the master even talked to her. But the woman had heard enough. She had been changed. She had been touched by Jesus and he had changed her entire life. Just like any other new Christian, she had to tell somebody. She left the waterpot. She did not need it anymore, she had Living Water and she would thirst no more. She did not need to come to the well again. Remember, most likely she was not really coming to the well for water, but rather she may have been coming for a man or a new lover. But now, she no longer had that need. Jesus took away her thirst for water and he also took away her thirst for another lover she would not marry.

The woman's initial reaction was no different than ours is today. As soon as we are fill or better stated overflowed with the Living Waters (the Holy Spirit) we want to go and tell someone. Most people we tell consider us to be a nuisance, but we still want to tell them. And it is ok to feel that way. The filling of the Holy Spirit fills your cup to the top with no room to add more. Yet, there is always more and we seem to want to find room within ourselves to add more. You are blessed both to be filled and to have room for more. That is a very strange fact. But do you remember Elijah and the woman at the gate gathering sticks? When Elijah asked her for bread, she responded:

And she said, As the LORD thy God liveth, I have not a cake, but an handful of meal in a barrel, and a little oil in a cruse:

I Am Come To Bring Living Water

and, behold, I am gathering two sticks, that I may go in and dress it for me and my son, that we may eat it, and die. And Elijah said unto her, Fear not; go and do as thou hast said: but make me thereof a little cake first, and bring it unto me, and after make for thee and for thy son. For thus saith the LORD God of Israel, The barrel of meal shall not waste, neither shall the cruse of oil fail, until the day that the LORD sendeth rain upon the earth. And she went and did according to the saying of Elijah: and she, and he, and her house, did eat many days. And the barrel of meal wasted not, neither did the cruse of oil fail, according to the word of the LORD, which he spake by Elijah. (1 Kings 17:12-16)

The barrel and the oil cruse did not fail for they were both almost empty and yet full as added by God. Or consider the feeding of the multitude (about 5000 thousand) by Christ with five loaves and two fishes or the 4000 thousand with seven loaves. Finally, consider the twenty-third Psalms and these words.

Thou preparest a table before me in the presence of mine enemies: thou anointest my head with oil; my cup runneth over. (Psalm 23:5)

The anointing is the filling of the Holy Spirit (Living Water) and notice it is poured on the David's head, but it fills his cup. Not just full, but running over the top. With the Living Water, you are full, it runs over, and there is still room to be filling again. So you are continually filled. That is why you will never thirst again.

Being so full, we almost explode with a desire to pour out this Living Water (Holy Spirit) on others. In fact Jesus said it will come out of our bellies.

He that believeth on me, as the scripture hath said, out of his belly shall flow rivers of living water. (John 7:38)

I Am Come To Bring Living Water

So it is expected you will want to tell somebody. Tell them, that is why you were filled with Living Water. It is your empowerment to spread the Gospel.

Jesus did one more remarkable thing with this woman many bible scholars overlook; he made her into the first and one of the greatest Gentile evangelical preachers. She was the first, because up until, *"And he must needs go through Samaria. (John 4:4)"*, Jesus had only gone to the Jews. The word of God was limited to Jews until that moment. For the first time Christ was shared with the Gentile and a woman preacher was called as a disciple and sent to preach the gospel to the Gentiles. And the woman at the well was truly an evangelical preacher. She went to town and shared her personal experience of meeting a man that knew all of her life (meaning her sins) to all the men and persuaded them to come and meet Christ. Her persuasion was *"is not this the Christ."* Why is she one of the greatest Gentile evangelical preachers?

> *Then they went out of the city, and came unto him. (John 4:30) And many of the Samaritans of that city believed on him for the saying of the woman, which testified, He told me all that ever I did. So when the Samaritans were come unto him, they besought him that he would tarry with them: and he abode there two days. (John 4:39-40)*

Only once in my life I have had the experience of evangelizing a whole city. It is difficult to know if you really attracted an audience made up of all the residence of a city, but you can know if the number of attendees in an audience exceeded the population of a city. And that is the experience I witness in a popular retirement city in Florida. It was a great joy to read a newspaper article that claimed the entire city attended a one night only revival meeting the previous night, especially when you were a part of the revival sponsoring ministry. But let me show you how much more significant was the evangelism of the woman at the well by comparing her accomplishments to the revival event I experienced in Florida.

I Am Come To Bring Living Water

First, this woman worked along. She only had Jesus and the Holy Ghost to help her evangelism activities. In Florida, I worked with four other ministers. In fact one of our drawing cards used to attract attention to the revival was come and hear five ministers preach as single sermon as one. We also had as much assistance as we requested. This included financial backing, parking ministry, master of ceremony, and one of the best music directors I know to lead the praise part of the revival. In most cases, we did not have to make requests, saints just volunteered where they saw a need.

Second, this woman preached her very short sermon in one afternoon to the men of the city and evangelized an entire city in time to return with the city's population to the well that same afternoon. In Florida, we worked an entire month in advance of the revival putting out flyers, going door to door, walking the beach, talking to everyone that would listen just to invite them to the one night only revival. Each and every day for that month, we walked the streets from early in the morning until late in the afternoon. We would go without eating in the day and go out for a large meal at the end of the day. We used the time of the meals to work on getting five men of God to agree on a single passage of scripture. You cannot have multiple ministers preach a single sermon as one unless they agree on the scripture as one. Let me tell you, it was very painful. I know the believers in Acts continued in prayer and were on one accord, so it is possible. But accomplishing one accord today is no small task. We struggled, but when we preached at that revival, if you closed your eyes, you could not tell who was speaking. Not only did we agree, but we came to sound alike. We were on one accord.

Third, her work resulted in the pure glorification of Jesus. Once they came to the well and heard Jesus, they no longer sought the woman or wished to hear her preaching. Instead they heard Jesus and believed because of Jesus. As much as I would have preferred a similar result in Florida, it did not happen. Everyone talked for months of the greatness of the revival and how wonderful an experience it had been. But they only spoke of the five ministers that spoke as one. They did not say they heard Jesus at the revival. They just heard the five ministers.

I Am Come To Bring Living Water

And many more believed because of his own word; And said unto the woman, Now we believe, not because of thy saying: for we have heard him ourselves, and know that this is indeed the Christ, the Saviour of the world. (John 4:41-42)

This result is the single goal of any teacher or preacher of the word of God. It is the task we were assigned to accomplish. I pray for the day men and women will come and tell me they believe because they have come to know Jesus themselves and no longer need to depend on the words I have spoken. They will proclaim they know Jesus and he is indeed the Christ, the Savior of the world. I know it is possible, because I have had students that obtained this level in Christ.

What did this woman offer that we ministers did not offer in Florida? The difference was the out pouring of Living Water. Sure we offered the Word of God, we taught Jesus, and we praise and glorified God, but I now understand it was not enough. The early church in the book of Act came on one accord, but then they waited as requested by Jesus to receive the Holy Ghost. And immediately after receiving the Holy Ghost, they experienced an out pouring of the Living Waters from there own bellies. What I am saying is it is not good enough to just minister the Word of God. For the Word of God without the Spirit of God is like an empty hope, a promise without commitment, or love without obedience. Simply stated, a seed once planted cannot grow without water. We have become experts in spreading the Word of God. We plant very well. But where are the water bearers? Who is bringing the water? If you just keep teaching the Word week after week and never pouring out the Living Water, it will become dry and fall away.

Preachers and teachers it is ok to stop teaching every now and then and let the Holy Ghost have his way. After people get so full of the Word, it is ok to pause and just praise God until the Spirit takes over and creates a new order of service. Maybe somebody will be touch, heal, or just comforted. But you have to back away from the desire to just preach or teach long enough to realize God has several other gifts the Holy Ghost may want to

71

use doing the previously appointed time for preaching and teaching. Just let it happen.

> *Trust in the LORD with all thine heart; and lean not unto thine own understanding. In all thy ways acknowledge him, and he shall direct thy paths. (Proverbs 3:5-6)*

What is Living Water?

Living Water is defined in one place in the bible. The definition was provided by Christ.

> *In the last day, that great day of the feast, Jesus stood and cried, saying, If any man thirst, let him come unto me, and drink. He that believeth on me, as the scripture hath said, out of his belly shall flow rivers of living water. (But this spake he of the Spirit, which they that believe on him should receive: for the Holy Ghost was not yet given; because that Jesus was not yet glorified.) (John 7:37-39)*

Jesus was now in Galilee and the feast of tabernacles was in its last day. That day was the Sabbath and this feast was special since it was the last feast of the year. The last day was a very joyous day and on this day, as was the practice each day of the festival, the priest carried water from the steam of Siloam (which flowed under the temple mountain) in golden vessels and poured it out on the altar. That was a very special high point of the day normally accompanied with jubilation. The people would sing:

> *Therefore with joy shall ye draw water out of the wells of salvation. (Isaiah 12:3)*

The trumpets were played and everyone was in great joy. At that moment, Jesus stood up and cried out in a loud voice, *"If any man thirst, let him come unto me, and drink. He that believeth on me as the scripture hath said, out of his belly shall flow rivers of living water."* If that happened in your church today, the usurers would come quickly and escort the speaker out the door as quietly as possible. In the minds of the church leaders, Jesus had not only disturbed the service right at its peak level, but he openly and publicly blasphemed God. They set their mind to Jesus had to go even if it meant his death. But as always, God's ways, God's thoughts are far from our ways and thoughts.

I Am Come To Bring Living Water

For as the heavens are higher than the earth, so are my ways higher than your ways, and my thoughts than your thoughts. (Isaiah 55:9)

Jesus was not speaking about the water from the well of Siloam. He was not speaking of a physical thirst. He was telling the entire feast of Jews the same message he gave to the woman at the well. He was offering the Living Water from his own belly. He was offering the Holy Spirit, the Comforter, and the Holy Ghost that was yet to come. That Spirit was already in the world and had been since the beginning of the world, but as of yet the Holy Spirit had not filled mankind and taken over as the guide and leader of our lives.

(But this spake he of the Spirit, which they that believe on him should receive: for the Holy Ghost was not yet given; because that Jesus was not yet glorified.) (John 7:39)

The key is Jesus offered the Living Water, the same Living Water he offered the woman at the well, but John now explains the Living Water is the Holy Spirit.

So now you understand my true calling. I am the bearer of Living Water. I am come to bring Living Water. The grass of a field, the lily of a valley and people will dry up and die without water. How much more so will your soul parish without the Living Water of life. I am not the creator of the Living Water and I am not the Living Water. I am just the bearer of the Living Water.

But whosoever drinketh of the water that I shall give him shall never thirst: but the water that I shall give him shall be in him a well of water springing up into everlasting life. (John 4:14)

I am the bearer of the Holy Spirit and so are you. I am come to bring the Spirit of God. I bring the spark, the unique connection, the overflowing of the Spirit. The grass of the field and the lily of the valley are just the saints of God. They have forsaken

I Am Come To Bring Living Water

the Living Waters. They have forsaken the Holy Spirit. They have turn from the guidance of God's Holy Spirit. Without this Spirit, their Christian walk will fall apart. It will dry up like a flower that gets no water. I am not the maker of the Holy Spirit and I am not the Holy Spirit. I am just another saint that has the Holy Spirit. I am just a bearer of the Holy Spirit. I am just a saint so full of the Holy Spirit it overflows out of my belly and if you come in contact with me, you will get a drink of this Living Water. I am called to fill you with the Holy Spirit until you over-flow and renew the Comforter in your life.

I Am Come To Bring Living Water

Principles of Living Water

Now that Living Water is defined, here are some basis principles you should understand about Living Water. This is not a complete listing of basis principles or laws of Living Water. Keep in mind Living Water is the Spirit of God. That Spirit continually adapts to guiding us in our every need. So there are not enough books on earth to contain all of the principles or laws of the Holy Spirit.

Comforter

Living Water is the Comforter requested by Jesus from God for us.

And I will pray the Father, and he shall give you another Comforter, that he may abide with you for ever; Even the Spirit of truth; whom the world cannot receive, because it seeth him not, neither knoweth him: but ye know him; for he dwelleth with you, and shall be in you. (John 14:16-17)

The Comforter is for those that love Christ and obey his commandments. The world can neither see nor know this Comforter. Therefore, the Living Water or the Holy Spirit which you can freely share with other believers can never fall into the hands of the unbelievers. Which means you can freely pour out your Spirit on the world and your pearls will never be received by swine. So why are some of you so reserved with the Holy Ghost? Why do many quench the Spirit? Only good can come from sharing the Holy Ghost.

But the natural man receiveth not the things of the Spirit of God: for they are foolishness unto him: neither can he know them, because they are spiritually discerned. (1 Corinthians 2:14)

76

I Am Come To Bring Living Water

Living Water or the Comforter will teach you what you need to know and do not know. He will also bring to you remembrance all you learned previously from Christ and the Word and forgot. He will cause you to remember again right at the time you need to know.

But the Comforter, which is the Holy Ghost, whom the Father will send in my name, he shall teach you all things, and bring all things to your remembrance, whatsoever I have said unto you. (John 14:26)

And when they bring you unto the synagogues, and unto magistrates, and powers, take ye no thought how or what thing ye shall answer, or what ye shall say: For the Holy Ghost shall teach you in the same hour what ye ought to say. (Luke 12:11-12)

So why are some of you afraid to speak up for the Lord? You will always know what to say because the Holy Spirit will give you the right words to speak. Jesus anticipated our fear and gave us the Living Water to be a comfort in our times of fear. Christ said it best.

Peace I leave with you, my peace I give unto you: not as the world giveth, give I unto you. Let not your heart be troubled, neither let it be afraid. (John 14:27)

Christ removed our fears, put our hearts as ease, and gave us the peace required to share his word with others. And what will you say to others. Well the Comforter already has instructions from Jesus as to what to bring to your remembrance or what to teach you to say.

But when the Comforter is come, whom I will send unto you from the Father, even the Spirit of truth, which proceedeth from the Father, he shall testify of me: (John 15:26)

I Am Come To Bring Living Water

I have yet many things to say unto you, but ye cannot bear them now. Howbeit when he, the Spirit of truth, is come, he will guide you into all truth: for he shall not speak of himself; but whatsoever he shall hear, that shall he speak: and he will shew you things to come. He shall glorify me: for he shall receive of mine, and shall shew it unto you. (John 16:12-14)

The Comforter will give testimony of Jesus. While Christ walked on the earth, he could teach of himself and his father. Now that he is with his father, it is job of the Comforter, the Living Water, the Holy Spirit to bring to remembrance what Christ taught and to teach us all we need to know about Christ and his father. That is why, when you read and study God's word, you should pray for understanding which is supplied by the Comforter.

The principle of the Father, Son, and Holy Spirit is made very simple when it comes to our relationship with the Holy Trinity. All three have been with mankind since the beginning. There are examples in many places in the Old Testament that mention the presence of the Holy Spirit and the son of God. Christ spoke many times of the presence of the Father and the Spirit. And the Father even spoke in the New Testament proclaiming his pleasure in his Son right after the Holy Spirit descended on Christ like a dove. So all three have always been here, but only one deals with mankind at any one time. In the Old Testament, God as the Father spoke to selected mankind. In the New Testament, Christ came in body form and spoke to select mankind as the son of God. And today, the Comforter has come and speaks to select mankind. Christ made it plain before he left and the message is also found in Acts.

Nevertheless I tell you the truth; It is expedient for you that I go away: for if I go not away, the Comforter will not come unto you; but if I depart, I will send him unto you. (John 16:7)

The former treatise have I made, O Theophilus, of all that Jesus began both to do and teach, Until the day in which he was

I Am Come To Bring Living Water

taken up, after that he through the Holy Ghost had given commandments unto the apostles whom he had chosen: (Acts 1:1-2)

So, what is the catch? Why did Jesus really give us a Comforter? Well Christ knew he would not reach the entire world in the three of so years he ministered. He knew the direct reach of his minister would not go near far enough. So Christ put in place a method to continue his ministry. He understood the principles of apostleship. He knew how to select disciples, teach them and then send them out as apostles. He knew they would do the same and their apostles would do the same. So he took a small unknown group of men and women and established a process that change the stone that was overlooked by the builders into the chief corner stone upon which he would build his church. So that is the catch. You have the Living Water, the Holy Spirit for one purpose and that is to witness.

Go ye therefore, and teach all nations, baptizing them in the name of the Father, and of the Son, and of the Holy Ghost: Teaching them to observe all things whatsoever I have commanded you: and, lo, I am with you alway, even unto the end of the world. Amen. (Matthew 28:19-20)

But ye shall receive power, after that the Holy Ghost is come upon you: and ye shall be witnesses unto me both in Jerusalem, and in all Judaea, and in Samaria, and unto the uttermost part of the earth. (Acts 1:8)

So you see Living Water is for the purpose of witnessing to the world. The Comforter is not come to make life easy for you. His job is not just to provide you comfort. His job is to provide you with the tools necessary to witness unto Jesus. So many Christian Churches like to speak of the Holy Spirit just as a comfort to our lives. These Christian Churches are generally silent about the baptism in the Spirit and the gifts of the Spirit. But the Comforter is not just a comfort for our lives. He is the third person of the Holy Trinity and his work is Christ's work. Both of their work is the salvation of the world. That is why God choose the seed of Abraham. He wanted to save the world and they were the chosen people to make it happen. And that is why he has chosen you and me today. He still wants to save the world. He will use the Gentiles if the Jews will not do the job.

Received the Living Water of Christ, but know the principle or law that these waters are for saving souls. Become aware of principles or laws related to Living Water or the Holy Spirit. Having knowledge of the principles or laws will aid you in the ministration of the Holy Spirit. Often, Christians do not exercise the power of Christ that is within them simply because they are unaware of nature of that power. In short, they have not studied the Word to understand the power of Holy Spirit. Now, that does not mean they do not read the Word of God or that they do not hear the Word of God preached. It simply means they have not studied or heard how the power of the Holy Spirit works. Here are a few more principles or laws about the Holy Spirit.

Just Ask for the Holy Spirit

Various Christian churches have ceremonial practices for the baptism of the Holy Spirit. Some churches will tell you it happens automatically at the time of water baptism. But I remind those churches it was not always the case in the book of Acts. Consider the converts under the hands of Phillip (one of the seven) in Samaria. Phillip preached and baptized. But it was not until Peter and John arrived that they laid hands on the converts to receive the Holy Spirit.

Then Philip went down to the city of Samaria, and preached Christ unto them. And the people with one accord gave heed unto those things which Philip spake, hearing and seeing the miracles which he did. For unclean spirits, crying with loud voice, came out of many that were possessed with them: and many taken with palsies, and that were lame, were healed. And there was great joy in that city. (Acts 8:5-8)

Now when the apostles which were at Jerusalem heard that Samaria had received the word of God, they sent unto them

I Am Come To Bring Living Water

Peter and John: Who, when they were come down, prayed for them, that they might receive the Holy Ghost: (For as yet he was fallen upon none of them: only they were baptized in the name of the Lord Jesus.) Then laid they their hands on them, and they received the Holy Ghost. (Acts 8:14-17)

Other churches as noted in the scriptures above, will lay hands on those to receive the Holy Spirit and pray. There are even some churches that will pray, shout, cry out, and perform several other acts for thirty minutes or more until those seeking the Holy Spirit began to speak in tongues. Sometimes it even takes several of those types of sessions.

Well here is where the scriptural principle or law is needed.

If ye then, being evil, know how to give good gifts unto your children: how much more shall your heavenly Father give the Holy Spirit to them that ask him? (Luke 11:13)

All you have to do to receive Holy Spirit is ask. There is no need for special ceremonies. There is no need for the laying on of hands. There are no special secret words or chants to speak. There is no need for saints with the Holy Spirit to be present when you ask. In fact you can be all along. This is why there are so many different examples of believers receiving the Holy Spirit in Act. It is because there is no set way to make it happen. When the wind blows, no man can tell where it comes from or where it goes. The Holy Spirit is the same. When I first received the Holy Spirit in my life with evidence of speaking in tongues, I was driving home from church by myself. I asked and God gave.

Also note there is no special order of events in the Holy Spirit. In fact, the opposite is generally true, there is normally no sense of what we call order when we follow the Holy Spirit. In the book of acts, there are examples of people receiving the Holy Spirit after water baptism, with water baptism, before water baptism, after formal acceptance of Christ and even before formal acceptance of Christ. The receipt of the Holy Spirit is sometimes in the book of Acts received on a one by one basis and sometimes received by a multitude all at once. The Holy Spirit is also received by all races, nations, and religious orders in the book of Acts.

The Holy Spirit declares Jesus as Lord

This is a very hard scriptural truth for many. It is contrary to what so many teach. I think not because they intend to teach in error, but rather they lack the knowledge of scriptural principles and laws about the Holy Spirit. When you really stand back and pray about this truth, the Holy Spirit will reveal it to you even if you have never read or studied the scripture. This scriptural principle or law is very hard to accept because of what it says about many Christians that lack the power to bind and loose on earth and about their acceptance of Jesus as their Savior.

It is not possible to declare Jesus as your Lord (κ□ριος or kyrios in Greek meaning Lord, Lordship, Master or Owner) without the Holy Ghost in you. Without the Holy Ghost, your declaration of Jesus as your Lord and Savior is just lying.

Wherefore I give you to understand, that no man speaking by the Spirit of God calleth Jesus accursed: and that no man can say that Jesus is the Lord, but by the Holy Ghost. (1 Corinthians 12:3)

I know many will say I must be taking this scriptural principle or law out of context, so here is a second scriptural example to make you believe.

When Jesus came into the coasts of Caesarea Philippi, he asked his disciples, saying, Whom do men say that I the Son of man am? And they said, Some say that thou art John the Baptist: some, Elias; and others, Jeremias, or one of the prophets. He saith unto them, But whom say ye that I am? And Simon Peter answered and said, Thou art the Christ, the Son of the living God. And Jesus answered and said unto him, Blessed art thou, Simon Barjona: for flesh and blood hath not revealed it unto thee, but my Father which is in heaven. And I say also unto thee, That thou art Peter, and upon this rock I will build my church; and the gates of hell shall not prevail

I Am Come To Bring Living Water

against it. And I will give unto thee the keys of the kingdom of heaven: and whatsoever thou shalt bind on earth shall be bound in heaven: and whatsoever thou shalt loose on earth shall be loosed in heaven. (Matthew 16:13-19)

Notice Christ told Peter flesh and blood did not reveal who he was, but his Father in Heaven told Peter and that Father is a Spirit, in fact the Holy Spirit. In teaching these scriptures several of us teachers become too involve in trying to explain the original church being founded or led by Peter as an indication of the church being built on the rock (which we define as Peter). But the true rock the church is built on is Jesus our Lord and the son of the living God. We cannot know this except by the Holy Spirit. What other forces than Jesus could stand against the gates of hell? Note the giving of the keys of the Kingdom of Heaven and power to bind and loose to a saint (Peter).

So it is only with the power of the Holy Ghost I can declare Jesus Christ as my Lord and Savior and gain the power to bind and loose on earth.

The way to enter the Kingdom of God

First, the Kingdom of Heaven and the Kingdom of God are used interchangeable in the scriptures and I agree they are the same. This Kingdom is here now and will continue eternally after this Heaven and Earth have passed away. The Kingdom is the place where Christ rules. The primary key to the ministry of Christ was to tell us how to enter this Kingdom. It is like showing us how to come home or how to ascend into the heavens, not just when this earthly life ends, but even now while we are trapped in this earthly life. But the key to entering the Kingdom of Heaven, the only way into the Kingdom of Heaven, is the Holy Spirit. You must be born again, not of flesh as before, but of Spirit. You must be baptized not just of water washing away sins, but of Spirit becoming a new creature that can boldly enter into the Kingdom of Heaven (a place where flesh and blood cannot enter).

I Am Come To Bring Living Water

There was a man of the Pharisees, named Nicodemus, a ruler of the Jews: The same came to Jesus by night, and said unto him, Rabbi, we know that thou art a teacher come from God: for no man can do these miracles that thou doest, except God be with him. Jesus answered and said unto him, Verily, verily, I say unto thee, Except a man be born again, he cannot see the kingdom of God. Nicodemus saith unto him, How can a man be born when he is old? can he enter the second time into his mother's womb, and be born? Jesus answered, Verily, verily, I say unto thee, Except a man be born of water and of the Spirit, he cannot enter into the kingdom of God. That which is born of the flesh is flesh; and that which is born of the Spirit is spirit. (John 3:1-6)

How can this be? How can a man be born again? When you hear the sound of the wind blowing, you cannot see the wind and tell where it came from or where it is going. But you know it is wind. The same is true of being born again of the Spirit or being baptized in the Spirit. You will not see where the Holy Spirit came from or where it is going, but you will know He entered your life. You also will not see where the Holy Spirit is going to lead you, but you will know you are in the Kingdom of Heaven when you go.

Marvel not that I said unto thee, Ye must be born again. The wind bloweth where it listeth, and thou hearest the sound thereof, but canst not tell whence it cometh, and whither it goeth: so is every one that is born of the Spirit. (John 3:7-8)

Ok, so the Holy Spirit is the entrance into the Kingdom of Heaven, but what about that power to bind and loose?

The Holy Spirit has signs
Just as you can hear the wind blow and not see it, you will see the signs of the receipt of the Holy Spirit and not know from where or when it came. In the book of Acts, time and time again, the receipt of the Holy Spirit is noted by signs and wonders. Most times it was the speaking in tongues, but not always. What

is important is there were almost always signs discussed. In fact in the cases where there are no words about the signs there are only the statements that someone received the Holy Spirit. I think in those cases there were actually signs, but they were not recorded by the author. Else, how would the author know the Holy Spirit was received? So Christ wants us to know someone has received the Holy Spirit. He told his followers to tarry or wait until they had received the Holy Spirit before they started witnessing. So they had to have some way of knowing when they got the Holy Spirit. The same is true for believers today.

And, being assembled together with them, commanded them that they should not depart from Jerusalem, but wait for the promise of the Father, which, saith he, ye have heard of me. For John truly baptized with water; but ye shall be baptized with the Holy Ghost not many days hence. (Acts 1:4-5)

So believers that are assisting other in being baptized in the Holy Spirit should expect the signs and tarry with the recipients until they see the signs. Those that are praying along to receive the Holy Spirit should expect and only believe they have received an answer to their prayer when they experience the signs. What are the signs? Paul listed several for us.

For to one is given by the Spirit the word of wisdom; to another the word of knowledge by the same Spirit; To another faith by the same Spirit; to another the gifts of healing by the same Spirit; To another the working of miracles; to another prophecy; to another discerning of spirits; to another divers kinds of tongues; to another the interpretation of tongues: But all these worketh that one and the selfsame Spirit, dividing to every man severally as he will. (1 Corinthians 12:8-11)

The outward display of these signs or gifts of the Spirit will bear witness of the receipt of the Holy Spirit. Here are several examples of such a witness in the book of Acts and Hebrews.

I Am Come To Bring Living Water

Acts   **2:4**   *(KJV)*
⁴ And they were all filled with the Holy Ghost, and began to speak with other tongues, as the Spirit gave them utterance.

Acts   **2:17-18**   *(KJV)*
¹⁷ And it shall come to pass in the last days, saith God, I will pour out of my Spirit upon all flesh: and your sons and your daughters shall prophesy, and your young men shall see visions, and your old men shall dream dreams: ¹⁸ And on my servants and on my handmaidens I will pour out in those days of my Spirit; and they shall prophesy:

Acts   **4:31**   *(KJV)*
³¹ And when they had prayed, the place was shaken where they were assembled together; and they were all filled with the Holy Ghost, and they spake the word of God with boldness.

Acts   **9:17**   *(KJV)*
¹⁷ And Ananias went his way, and entered into the house; and putting his hands on him said, Brother Saul, the Lord, even Jesus, that appeared unto thee in the way as thou camest, hath sent me, that thou mightest receive thy sight, and be filled with the Holy Ghost.

Acts   **10:47**   *(KJV)*
⁴⁷ Can any man forbid water, that these should not be baptized, which have received the Holy Ghost as well as we?

Acts   **11:15**   *(KJV)*
¹⁵ And as I began to speak, the Holy Ghost fell on them, as on us at the beginning.

Acts   **13:52**   *(KJV)*
⁵² And the disciples were filled with joy, and with the Holy Ghost.

I Am Come To Bring Living Water

Acts   *15:8*   *(KJV)*
[8] And God, which knoweth the hearts, bear them witness, giving them the Holy Ghost, even as he did unto us;

Acts   *19:6*   *(KJV)*
[6] And when Paul had laid his hands upon them, the Holy Ghost came on them; and they spake with tongues, and prophesied.

Hebrews   *2:4*   *(KJV)*
[4] God also bearing them witness, both with signs and wonders, and with divers miracles, and gifts of the Holy Ghost, according to his own will?

There are many that refer to the teachings of Paul in 1 Corinthians 12 – 14 as an indication we should never seek or even expect an outpouring of Spiritual gifts. I disagree. I believe the gifts operate as a sign of the power of the Holy Spirit to us and to the unbeliever. I believe these signs are necessary even today, maybe even more so today, that we and the world will believe in the power of the Holy Spirit and in Christ. The enemy has gotten us to back away from these powers to turn his arguments against Christ and to what seems to be logic. But with the signs, we defy logic because Spirit is not logical. Do not allow the enemy the opportunity to steal your power in Christ. Look closely at what Paul taught.

Now there are diversities of gifts, but the same Spirit. And there are differences of administrations, but the same Lord. And there are diversities of operations, but it is the same God which worketh all in all. But the manifestation of the Spirit is given to every man to profit withal. For to one is given by the Spirit the word of wisdom; to another the word of knowledge by the same Spirit; To another faith by the same Spirit; to another the gifts of healing by the same Spirit; To another the working of miracles; to another prophecy; to another discerning of spirits; to another divers kinds of tongues; to another the interpretation of tongues: But all these worketh that one and the selfsame Spirit, dividing to every man severally as he will. (1 Corinthians 12:4-11)

Many bible teachers indicate this charter followed by the chapter on love and then chapter fourteen where Paul clearly expresses his preference to only seek gifts that edify the church as a whole is an indication to not seek the outward signs of the receipt of the Holy Spirit such as speaking in tongues. But look closely at chapter fourteen and notice each time you find the word "spirit" it is spelled with a small "s". This signifies Paul is speaking of the spirit in man and not the Holy Spirit of God. So his entire instruction deals with how we work in the church with our own spirits and not how the Holy Spirit works in the church. Note in the twelfth chapter, Paul uses the large "S" with all but one use of the word "Spirit". The receipt of the Holy Spirit should always be noted by gifts of the Spirit as signs.

Forget the flesh
Once you are baptized in the Spirit, you will forget things of the flesh. You will loose the desires of the flesh. You are a different person. In fact, you are a new born again person that is no longer flesh and blood, but that is Spirit. You literally become a son of God. That means you are part of the body of Christ (like his arm or leg). You can enter the Kingdom of God because you are no longer yourself, but part of the body of Christ. The two of you have become one flesh one body, and one person.

Therefore, brethren, we are debtors, not to the flesh, to live after the flesh. For if ye live after the flesh, ye shall die: but if ye through the Spirit do mortify the deeds of the body, ye shall live. For as many as are led by the Spirit of God, they are the sons of God. For ye have not received the spirit of bondage again to fear; but ye have received the Spirit of adoption, whereby we cry, Abba, Father. The Spirit itself beareth witness with our spirit, that we are the children of God: (Romans 8:12-16)

I Am Come To Bring Living Water

Free from death

Every since the first sin in the Garden of Eden, man has been curse to die due to sin, but with the Baptism of the Spirit, you are made free from that curse. Before, if you sinned you would surely die just as foretold as the penalty for Adam's eating of the tree of knowledge of good and evil. But with the receipt of the Holy Spirit you have a new life and you are free to partake of the tree of life that was also in the Garden of Eden, but was not eating. And now, you will no longer see death.

Here are a couple scriptures on how the Holy Spirit frees you from death. But I think it takes more than these scriptures to really understand this principle.

There is therefore now no condemnation to them which are in Christ Jesus, who walk not after the flesh, but after the Spirit. For the law of the Spirit of life in Christ Jesus hath made me free from the law of sin and death. (Romans 8:1-2)

Now the Lord is that Spirit: and where the Spirit of the Lord is, there is liberty. (2 Corinthians 3:17)

So what does that really mean? How am I freed from death? And what does that freedom mean in terms of how I am to live for Christ?

When you are under the binding of the law, your actions are limited to those that are allowed within the law. If the speed limit on the road is 30 miles an hour, you are free to drive any safe speed between 0 and 30 miles an hour. But you are not free to operate outside those limits. So you continually or frequently check your speed because you continually or frequently fear the violation of the law. What Christ gave us is not the opportunity to not obey the law, but rather the freedom from the fear of disobeying the law. He gave us a peace from that fear. So you can finally stop continually or frequently checking the speed you are traveling to assure you do not disobey the law. The freedom from the fear or the peace from the fear is the elimination of the penalty for violating the law. It is the elimination of the curse of death to all that disobey the law. What Christ gave us is, "we will not surely die if we sin against the law".

After the resurrection of Christ, he was seen several times by his disciples and greeted them with the words "peace be unto you". For example,

> *And as they thus spake, Jesus himself stood in the midst of them, and saith unto them, Peace be unto you. (Luke 24:36)*

Other examples are found in John 20: 19, 21, and 26. This peace was not offered before the resurrection because this peace was an assurance death no longer had its grip on the saints. This peace was a peace or freedom from the fear of the retribution of the law. This freedom is within the believers and it comes from the Holy Spirit within us. I am not freed so I can disobey the law, but instead I am freed so I can obey the Holy Spirit. So this is how I overcome the struggle inside of me that Paul speaks of in Roman 7. I quit the fight within me between good and evil; I quit trying to do good while evil is ever present and simple found peace by following and obeying the Holy Spirit. The Holy Spirit frees me from death for disobeying the law. For when I obey the Holy Spirit, I cannot and will not disobey the law.

> *These things have I spoken unto you, being yet present with you. But the Comforter, which is the Holy Ghost, whom the Father will send in my name, he shall teach you all things, and bring all things to your remembrance, whatsoever I have said unto you. Peace I leave with you, my peace I give unto you: not as the world giveth, give I unto you. Let not your heart be troubled, neither let it be afraid. (John 14:25-27)*

And how should this peace that comes with the Holy Sprint work in my life from day to day to overcome death, the penalty of sin?

> *Rejoice in the Lord alway: and again I say, Rejoice. Let your moderation be known unto all men. The Lord is at hand. Be careful for nothing; but in every thing by prayer and suppli-*

cation with thanksgiving let your requests be made known unto God. And the peace of God, which passeth all understanding, shall keep your hearts and minds through Christ Jesus. Finally, brethren, whatsoever things are true, whatsoever things are honest, whatsoever things are just, whatsoever things are pure, whatsoever things are lovely, whatsoever things are of good report; if there be any virtue, and if there be any praise, think on these things. Those things, which ye have both learned, and received, and heard, and seen in me, do: and the God of peace shall be with you. (Philippians 4:4-9)

The joy of the Holy Ghost

I have always been troubled by churches that have a quiet, silent, and in awed spiritual worship experience. Maybe I am wrong, but when I read the Psalms, I just do not see the same quiet silent praise. Maybe I am just a loud mouth. But when I wonder what it will be like to stand and offer continual praises to God for all eternity, I just do not get a vision of people standing before God with their arms up in the air in silence. I mean, even the singing we do today on earth is louder than many of those quiet churches feel is appropriate in the presence of God. A joyful noise is just that. It is a noise and not a quiet silent praise. I think some of those quiet silent churches are just lacking the joy of the Holy Ghost. This joy is very important. It is required to enter into the Kingdom of God. Without the joy, there is no Kingdom of God, because the joy in the Holy Ghost is the Kingdom of God.

For the kingdom of God is not meat and drink; but righteousness, and peace, and joy in the Holy Ghost. (Romans 14:17)

The word "joy" is "chara" in the Greek. Vine translates it as "Gladness, Greatly, Joy, Joyfulness, Joyfully, Joyous" in Strong's Talking Greek & Hebrew Dictionary. That dictionary also defines "chara" as coming from the word "chario" which means cheerfulness or delight, such as gladness with greatly or exceeding joyfulness. So where is the quiet silent praise in that?

I Am Come To Bring Living Water

Many believers think there is such as thing as an appropriate way to act in church worship service. They think some of the excited loud expressions of select Christian are totally out of place. Most of these same believers think things like clapping of hands, stumping of feet, or dancing of any kind is out of place in the house of God. To those believers, I say, each of these activities is mentioned in the bible as format of praise. I also warn them they should not set up requirements or rules (better called laws) for how one should worship. If you set up such laws, you will be held accountable by God for obedience of such laws. Is it not better to allow the Holy Spirit to decide what is and what is not praise? Since following the Holy Spirit requires my giving up my ways and my thinking, then I should not expect to understand the worship directed by the Holy Spirit. In fact, I would expect worship directed by the Holy Spirit to not be in accordance with what I see, smell, taste, feel, or hear. I would expect true worship in the Spirit to be something outside of my understanding. So it may just be loud.

I know God can hear even a whisper, but maybe the real issue is the quiet, silent churches members can not hear the true praises to God because they are not loud enough. So my pray is this:

Now the God of hope fill you with all joy and peace in believing, that ye may abound in hope, through the power of the Holy Ghost. (Romans 15:13)

I was a member of various marching bands while in school. I played with two different high school bands and with a college band. In college, I was one of the very rare non music majors in the band. All male music major students were required to take the course for the band membership (which was an all male band at my Big Ten college), but I had no such requirement placed on me and yet I was a member because I enjoyed the marching band experience. I can play several woodwind instruments. The main interest of the marching band was to support the football team at games. So I generally attended all football games and many basketball games since I also played in the band for those games. The one thing I remember about the games is the loud cheers.

I Am Come To Bring Living Water

When you are in a stadium of 20,000 plus, the sound of everyone cheering is one of the loudest thing you will ever hear. People seem happiest when their team is winning and they are cheering them on. No one seems to mind how loud it gets, how cold the winter air feels, how foolishly some are dressed in support of their teams, how much this event really cost, or how much time it takes to enjoy this simple pleasure. People just put all of those common sense things aside and enjoy the game. The same is true when people watch key games on television such as the supper bowl.

But the same is not true for the ways of God. I have yet to see the same loud cheering in the church I use to see in the football stadium. I do not know, maybe I just have yet to go to the right church. But I have a problem with Christians that will cheer louder at a football game than at a church. Especially when those Christian tell me they are being quiet because they are being reverent to God. I have always wanted to give my best praises to God. It is like giving an offering. I always want to give my first fruits and my best fruits to God. So do not frown on me if I get too loud for you in Church. I am just trying to make sure I am giving my best praise to God. When I note the presence of the Holy Ghost in our service, I rejoice with exceeding joy. I cannot keep quiet. I know God can get his praise from so many others (such as angels or even stones). I know God enjoys the praise and I want to make sure I am found worthy to offer praise now and forever. Think of it this way, if God were looking for someone to stand in his presence and offer him praise continually, would he select you? Have you demonstrated a talent for praising God while you are on this earth? Are your praises to God so sweet he will want to hear them eternally? I do not know how I would fare in that test, but I will do all I can to please God as best I can with my praises and hope he finds them worthy enough to make me part of those saints that will praise him forever. And that is my joy in the Holy Ghost. It is a joy of praising God. No matter what is going on in my life and no matter if I am up or down, I can still by the power of the Holy Ghost steal away from my life and praise God. And when I began to praise, the joy comes.

I Am Come To Bring Living Water

For the kingdom of God is not meat and drink; but righteous-
ness, and peace, and joy in the Holy Ghost. (Romans 14:17)

<u>Seals and sanctifies</u>

The early church Christians shortly after the resurrection of
Christ often taught about being sealed by Christ. It was an experience they sometimes associated with water baptism or with
the baptism in the Spirit. It was believed, and I will also make
known in these writing once changed and sealed, a saint can no
longer regress to sin. In fact, once seal, there remained no further
opportunity for repentance if you once again fall into sin. That is
a very hard lesson and I will take a little while longer to build to
that level of spiritual knowledge. But for now, Saints should understand the need to become sealed and sanctified by the Living
Waters (Holy Spirit).

In whom ye also trusted, after that ye heard the word of truth,
the gospel of your salvation: in whom also after that ye be-
lieved, ye were sealed with that holy Spirit of promise, (Ephe-
sians 1:13)

And grieve not the holy Spirit of God, whereby ye are sealed
unto the day of redemption. (Ephesians 4:30)

So you were baptized in water. It symbolizes your cleansing
from all sin. All sins of your life were removed and put so far
from you God can no longer remembers them. But what will
keep you? What will make you remain sinless? How will you
live in this world full of sin and yet sin not? You cannot do it
without being sealed by the Holy Spirit.

The power of the Holy Spirit becomes like a wall between the
sins of the world all around us and the saint we are within. That
is what is meant by the guidance or the teaching of all things to
come provided by the Comforter (the Holy Spirit). Not that the
Holy Spirit will stop you from sinning. You have and will always have your own will. But the Holy Spirit offers awareness,
guidance, council, knowledge, and understanding of the danger

of sin. He offers these at a time of need, even if we fail to recognize the need. The Holy Spirit is like a small, still voice within us that provides warning and instruction as to how to flee the sin every time we are tempted to sin. The key is to hear the Holy Spirit and obey to avoid the sin.

I adopted a young boy years ago to provide him with an opportunity to attend school. The young man ran away from home and was just another drifter in Florida. He came to my attention, because he was under aged. He was 15 at the time and should have still been in school. I was running a center for transits that offered free room and board for up to three days, to allow a transit time to find employment and low income housing while living off the street. This young man obtained our phone number from the local police. He was told to call us to get off the street or be arrested and held in jail until they contacted his family. So he decided to call us. I picked him up and quickly developed an interest in helping him further than what was provided by the center. Since we had the space, I allowed him to stay longer. It was winter and the number of transit in Florida always declines in colder weather. In fact, at the time I already had two other center residences that were allowed to overstay the three day limit.

So since he was school age, he needed to be in school. With some investigation, I discovered he could not enroll in school unless he had a legal guardian living in Florida. So I took the steps and became his legal guardian so he could go to school. To my great surprise, that process only took about one month. His family (which only consisted of a one grandmother, a younger bother and sister) were given the opportunity to object, but instead decided to concur with the legal guardianship. So I got the young man in school and began the process of trying to change a 15 year old from the ways of the world to the ways of the Lord. Now, you and I both know such a change is rejected if you simply preach Jesus. So I used the method of showing the young man a Christ like life to emulate. I became his example.

Over the next 10 or more years, I was the parent that got the call when trouble occurred. And trouble occurred frequently. It ranged from fights, to playing hockey from school, to stealing, to drinking, to youth detention, and to even a short time in county jail. But do not think only the worst, for in the end, the young man developed in to a well balance father of three and husband of a good wife. It took a long time and often looked like a failure, but ended in success. He even reconciled with his younger brother and sister and became an aid to them.

One thing I remember about this young man. When ever he was considering doing something that was wrong or against the example I set before him, he would stop and talk to me first. Sometimes, a strange conversation at home, other times a strange call while I was at work that seemed to be about nothing, but was really a cry for help. It took me a little while to recognize the cries for help, but once I understood, I responded with "do not do it". I would never find out what "it" was until after the fact, but I always knew in my spirit "it" was wrong. It took some years of such warnings, counsel, advice, and guidance along with the help of a great alcohol counselor to turn the young man, but in the end he did learn to listen and accept the warnings, counsel, advice, and guidance.

The same is true with the seal of the Holy Spirit. He will continue to provide you with warnings, counsel, advice, and guidance at the time of need until we listen. He will provide guidance even when we are not aware of our own need for guidance. Our job is to learn to listen and grow in grace to the point we start seeking his guidance long before we are faced with the need. This last state of seeking guidance long before we are faced with the need is true sanctification. Most people think of being sanctified as be made pure, sinless, and prefect in the sight of God. And that is true, but the question is not what is sanctified, but how to become sanctified. It is not something I just pray for and it happens. It is not just saying the words out of your mouth without actions to back the words. And it is not just getting so old I can no longer physically do the sins of my youth and therefore decide to declare myself to be sanctified. No it is moving from being trapped by the temptation of sin and needing the help of the Holy Spirit to escape to seeking the help of the Holy Spirit before I start so I will not become trapped. It is one thing to not yield to temptation to sin, but it is a far better thing to never be tempted. I know Christ was tempted, but he was only tempted when lead by the Holy Spirit into the wilderness to be tempted. That happened so he would prove to us we can be tempted and yet overcome. But from that day forward, Christ was not tempted by the Devil. He was tempted by man and even called a man tempting him "Satin", but he was not tempted by the Devil. You too can stop the temptations of the Devil, man, and the world. Just make the Lord's Prayer a reality.

And lead us not into temptation, but deliver us from evil: For thine is the kingdom, and the power, and the glory, for ever. Amen. (Matthew 6:13)

Seek the Holy Spirit to lead you away from temptation. It is far better to not be tempted than to be tempted and sin not. For this reason you are sanctified by the Holy Spirit. It is not it will make you not able to sin, but it will keep you free from the temptation to sin. Therefore, seek to become sanctified by the Holy Ghost.

That I should be the minister of Jesus Christ to the Gentiles, ministering the gospel of God, that the offering up of the Gentiles might be acceptable, being sanctified by the Holy Ghost. (Romans 15:16)

Let me add one additional comment on sanctification. I have heard most of my life from many Christians sanctification means to "set apart as or declared holy." That is a definition, but it is the English dictionary definition. To truly understand the biblical definition, look into the Greek word that was translated into "sanctified". It is the word "□γι□ζω" translated as "hagiazo" and it means "to make holy, purify or consecrate, and to venerate". Being sanctified by the Holy Ghost is not being set apart. It is being made again this time as holy, consecrated, and purified. It is the work of the Holy Spirit in us and not some work we have already done on our own making us worthy to be set aside. Man cannot sanctify himself or anyone else. Only God by the power of the Holy Spirit can sanctify. God does not declare us holy, he makes us holy. Given that becoming sanctified is an act of the

I Am Come To Bring Living Water

Holy Ghost, I would become very careful about making testimonial declarations stating "I have been sanctified and filled with the Holy Ghost." If the Holy Ghost has not done or completed the work in us, then we are lying and lying against the Holy Ghost. You can find physical evidence of being filled with the Holy Ghost (fruits of the spirit and spiritual gifts), but I know of no evidence of sanctification noted in the scriptures. Once the work of sanctification is completed and you are Holy, then you may come before the present of the Lord in the Holiest of Holy in the Heavenly tabernacle. In other words, you can go home to heaven and rest. I know sanctification work is not completed in me, because I am still here on earth.

Spreads God's love abroad
We all love to quote John 3:16.

For God so loved the world, that he gave his only begotten Son, that whosoever believeth in him should not perish, but have everlasting life. (John 3:16)

We are all commission to carry this love of God to entire world.

Go ye therefore, and teach all nations, baptizing them in the name of the Father, and of the Son, and of the Holy Ghost: Teaching them to observe all things whatsoever I have commanded you: and, lo, I am with you alway, even unto the end of the world. Amen. (Matthew 28:19-20)

Or perhaps you prefer the words in Acts.

But ye shall receive power, after that the Holy Ghost is come upon you: and ye shall be witnesses unto me both in Jerusalem, and in all Judaea, and in Samaria, and unto the uttermost part of the earth. (Acts 1:8)

I Am Come To Bring Living Water

But did you know the only way to spread the love of John 3:16 from one heart to another abroad is with the power of the Holy Ghost.

And hope maketh not ashamed; because the love of God is shed abroad in our hearts by the Holy Ghost which is given unto us. (Romans 5:5)

You cannot share the love of God with someone in the world unless the Holy Ghost opens their heart to receive the love of God. Try all you want, but without the Holy Ghost, you will just sound like a loud clanging cymbal. When saints talk about Jesus knocking on the door of someone's heart with the message of salvation, they really mean the Holy Ghost is trying to open that person's heart so they can feel the love of God and hear the words of salvation. God's love is not like the love of man. Our love, even our attempts to show agape love are only physical. Man can only operate in the natural senses of touching, feeling, seeing, smelling, hearing, and tasting. But God's love is not expressed in those senses. God's agape love is spiritual because God is a spirit. Therefore it can only spread between people spiritually.

I do my own grocery shopping. It is one of those tasks I never look forward to doing. I simply do not enjoy shopping of any kind. But if I want to eat, it must be done. I pray a lot in super markets just to increase my enjoyment while I shop. I pray for others, not for myself. I pray for the lady that rides down the isle, because she cannot walk the isles. I pray for the parent that is frustrated by trying to control small children in the store. I pray a lot about the prices when I see people standing looking at the prices in total disbelief. One of my more exciting experiences is to see a little child, sometimes even the ones riding in the charts. I look at them and start praying for the success of their lives. These small children will face so much as they grow into adults. They need someone to pray for them. It is why Jesus suffered the little ones to come to him. Every now and then, the child becomes aware of my prayer. They cannot hear it, it is silent. They cannot see it, because I am not even moving my lips.

I Am Come To Bring Living Water

The only physical evidence is I am looking at them. But that is the power of the Holy Ghost. It is so powerful even a small child or a baby can become aware of Holy Ghost being directed to their lives. Watch them, they will become very shy, hide behind their parent and peep out back to me, or they will just smile or even wave at the stranger passing by that left them much more than a smile. The stranger left them the effectual prayers of the righteous and the Holy Ghost made them aware of that prayer. That is how the love of God moves from one heart to another. It is a completely spiritual movement. There is nothing physical about it. But you will know it happened, because the same Holy Spirit will confirm it in your heart.

As I mentioned before, I have had a few occasions to talk and pray with people just before they died. Their deaths were expected. If you every take up the ministry of visiting and comforting the sick, you will have some of these experiences. When ever you assist in leading a soul to Christ at a time near death, you always want to know your work is completed. You want to know they are really accepting Jesus into their lives. You know deep down inside, if they fail to respond to this opportunity, there will not be any other opportunities for that dying person to be saved from eternal damnation. So how do you know? These things are spiritual and not physical. You will not see the evidence and you cannot always trust what you hear from the person. It is not the kind of thing you can feel physically. But instead, the spirit of God inside of you must bear witness the dying soul in front of you has accepted the Lord Jesus. And when that happens, there is no fear inside of you it is not true. You will find you are willing to proclaim to the world, the sick person in front of you has really accepted the Lord Jesus. The assurance you will have in your heart is just as assure you are you have Jesus in your life. Then you know, that you know, that you know they are saved and will soon be going home to be with the Lord.

Let me try to explain how you know again. The Holy Spirit has always provided signs and wonders to support the truth of the word of God. So within John 3:16 is the very key phase, "*believeth in him*". This phase is the basis of the transformation that takes place in the non believer that results in there becoming a believer. I have already explained it takes place spiritually. But what happens in the physical after the spiritual event one may note not so much as evidence or substance, but rather as a fact of a different life. Since a new life begins with that belief, then it should be a different life. Here are things that will change as noted in the scriptures.

o The new life in Christ will not perish. This is not the kind of thing you can see, but the kind of thing that will be revealed over time.

And as Moses lifted up the serpent in the wilderness, even so must the Son of man be lifted up: (John 3:14)

He that <u>believeth on him</u> is not condemned: but he that believeth not is condemned already, because he hath not believed in the name of the only begotten Son of God. (John 3:18)

o The new life in Christ is remitted of all sins. This you will see because the fear of death is removed. Since there is no condemnation (or death) because all sin is forgiven, you will notice the new freedom in the new life in Christ. It is the same freedom Christ had from following the law while he walked the face of the earth. The Pharisee assumed he violated the law, but in reality he was freed from the penalty of the law.

To him give all the prophets witness, that through his name whosoever <u>believeth in him</u> shall receive remission of sins. (Acts 10:43)

o The new life in Christ will not be confounded (put to shame, disgrace, or dishonor). You will note the new life is all at once no longer ashamed of itself. Because it is no longer burden by the wrongs it did in the passed, it is all at once freed from all shame and disgrace.

I Am Come To Bring Living Water

Wherefore also it is contained in the scripture, Behold, I lay in Sion a chief corner stone, elect, precious: and he that believeth on him shall not be confounded. (1 Peter 2:6)

So what I am saying is the sick person you are witnessing to just before natural death will change if they accept Christ. And change will be noted spiritually in your heart. It will also show signs in the physical because that sick person will realize they and not dying, but instead beginning a new life. They will be freed from the burden of sin and its wages for the first time in their life. And that freedom or release of burdens will be visible to all that look on as a unique peace that was not present before. And most of all, there will be no shame. It is like having no regrets for the life they have lived. For all of there regrets have been forgiven and there is no wrong to be ashamed of left. And that is how the Love of God is spread abroad in our hearts by the Holy Ghost.

Blasphemy against the Holy Ghost

Wherefore I say unto you, All manner of sin and blasphemy shall be forgiven unto men: but the blasphemy against the Holy Ghost shall not be forgiven unto men. And whosoever speaketh a word against the Son of man, it shall be forgiven him: but whosoever speaketh against the Holy Ghost, it shall not be forgiven him, neither in this world, neither in the world to come. (Matthew 12:31-32)

Now I come to the hard teachings. This principle and the next one I will explain are very hard to accept. That is because they will limit the capabilities of the believer. Everything that has a beginning also has an end. Teachers often discuss in Christ the beginning and the end are one in the same and they really are one in the same. This world started with one Adam in perfect union with God before the first sin and it will end with one body in Christ in perfect union with God. The good news is we Christians will be a part of that one body of Christ since the church is the body of Christ. But rest assured there will be an end to all things including the period of time for grace.

Most bible teachers approaching the verse 31 – 32 of Matthew will quickly tell you the bible teaches all sins are forgivable. Then they are in a paradox, because the verse very plainly states, *"blasphemy against the Holy Ghost shall not be forgiven unto men"*. Just in case you missed the meaning, it is directly followed by *"And whosoever speaketh a word against the Son of man, it shall be forgiven him: but whosoever speaketh against the Holy Ghost, it shall not be forgiven him, neither in this world, neither in the world to come."* So most bible teachers then began a long explanation of how God can both forgive all sins and yet not forgive this sin. They normally end with there is something very unique about the way one blasphemy against the Holy Ghost that causes it to be an unforgivable sin. For example several state the blasphemer is challenging the authority of God by how they present their blasphemy. Well I am a lot simpler in my teaching and I simply state all sins are forgivable, but there is a limit as to how many times even God will forgive the same offense. That simple statement contains the truth about blasphemy against the Holy Ghost. Let me explain.

Remember this question from Peter.

Then came Peter to him, and said, Lord, how oft shall my brother sin against me, and I forgive him? till seven times? Jesus saith unto him, I say not unto thee, Until seven times: but, Until seventy times seven. (Matthew 18:21-22)

Or consider the similar scripture in Luke.

Take heed to yourselves: If thy brother trespass against thee, rebuke him; and if he repent, forgive him. And if he trespass against thee seven times in a day, and seven times in a day turn again to thee, saying, I repent; thou shalt forgive him. (Luke 17:3-4)

Notice in both cases, Jesus did not instruct his disciples to forgive eternally, but instead there is a definite end to the number of times you should forgive your brother. Jesus used these examples to explain how God forgives us similarly. In fact he was making the point that if we start failing to forgive our brother repetitively, then God will start failing to forgive us repetitively. But in every case, there is an end to the matter of forgiveness. Forgiveness is not endless. If it were endless, then we would be able to continue to seek forgiveness even after our death in this world. And we all know that is not possible. If you die with sins that are not confessed and forgiven, then there is no further opportunity to confess and seek forgiveness of those sins after death.

The scriptures show God to be very long suffering. God will put up with our sinful nature for a long time and he will forgive us time and time again even for the repeat of the same sin over and over again. But rest assured, there is an end to even the patience of God. There is a time when he will no longer forgive us. I think God showed that type response with Sodom and Gomorrah. God allow there sins to go on for some time. And even after he sent his angels to destroy the city, he still heard and honored the request of Abram to save the city if ten righteous are found in the cities. But once ten were not found, then the Lord's patience and forgiveness ended and he destroyed the cities. The key is all things of this world must at some time by the seasons of the Lord come to an end.

This is also true of God's plan for our salvation. At one time, there was Adam without sin and God and man were one. Sin separated God from Adam and created the wages of sin, which is death. Note death did not exist prior to the first sin. The Law was put in place to show man salvation, but the Law was too great a task master to be conquered by man. We failed to find salvation under the Law. Then Jesus, who freed us from the bondage or the penalty of the Law, showed us salvation by God's love, grace, and his sacrifice for our salvation. All we had to do was believe. After Jesus' resurrection, he gave us the Holy Spirit as a Comforter, guide, and the tool we would need to save the world by the preaching of Jesus Christ. Now brothers and sisters, there is nothing else that will come after the Holy Spirit. It is God's last and final attempt to give us salvation. If we fail to accept this final gift from God, there remain no further opportunities. In other words, if you denied the law, then denied Jesus, and now you deny or turn down the Holy Spirit, there is no further opportunity for forgiveness and salvation. More simply, you can speak evil of the God, the Law, and even Jesus, but if you also speak evil of the Holy Spirit, there is no other forgiveness opportunity left.

> *Wherefore I say unto you, All manner of sin and blasphemy shall be forgiven unto men: but the blasphemy against the Holy Ghost shall not be forgiven unto men. And whosoever speaketh a word against the Son of man, it shall be forgiven him: but whosoever speaketh against the Holy Ghost, it shall not be forgiven him, neither in this world, neither in the world to come. (Matthew 12:31-32)*

You are only filled once

Just like the message on blasphemy, there is also a similar message on being filled with the Holy Spirit. It is appointed to man to only be filled with the Holy Spirit once. If you turn back after being filled (in a sense rejecting the Holy Spirit that is within you), then there is no further opportunity to be filled with the Holy Spirit again.

> *For it is impossible for those who were once enlightened, and have tasted of the heavenly gift, and were made partakers of the Holy Ghost, And have tasted the good word of God, and the powers of the world to come, If they shall fall away, to renew them again unto repentance; seeing they crucify to themselves the Son of God afresh, and put him to an open shame. (Hebrews 6:4-6)*

If you turn back after coming this far, then to renew you again is to put Christ on the cross again and to say his dying once for all our sins was not enough. It is like saying his sacrifice of his life was useless. That is the open shame you would place on Christ.

I Am Come To Bring Living Water

So similar to the teaching on blasphemy, turning your back on gift of God after you have been filled with the Holy Ghost, partaken in the heavenly gifts of the Spirit, and received and feasted on the word of God and its powers makes it impossible to be forgiven and be re-baptized, re-born again, and refilled by the Holy Spirit. As I stated before all things in this world must come to an end and the Holy Spirit is the end of God's plan for your salvation. After that end, there is only waiting for judgment. The Hebrew author said it this way.

For the earth which drinketh in the rain that cometh oft upon it, and bringeth forth herbs meet for them by whom it is dressed, receiveth blessing from God: But that which beareth thorns and briers is rejected, and is nigh unto cursing; whose end is to be burned. (Hebrews 6:7-8)

When it rains on the earth, the seeds in the ground bring forward plants after its kind. Some are good for food and some are not. The judgment of good and bad is performed. Those that are not good for food are gathered and cast into the fire. It will be the same with all that receive Living Water. Some will be saints and some will be non saints. After judgment, the non saints will be cast into the fires of hell.

Maybe, there are better ways to teach the lessons on blasphemy and rejecting the Holy Spirit after you have tasted it fruits, but sometimes the simply truth is the best way to communicate.

Fruit Of The Spirit

Every seed planted that takes root, receives water, and sun light should grow into its own kind. If it is not choked away by other plants and if it does not weather from too much sun light, it should grow. When it is a seed and when it is small, you can not always tell what kind of plant it will become. Once it is grown, it will bear fruit. By its fruit you should be able to discern the type of plant or its kind. The Laws of God, sometimes called the laws of nature by non Christians, assure an apple tree will bear the fruit of apples; a peach tree will bear the fruit of peaches, and so on. Those same Laws assure apple trees only bear fruit of its kind so you do not get peaches from apple trees. In addition, those Laws cause the bearing of fruit to multiple. Such that a single apple tree seed may grow in multiple trees with several branches and a greater multitude of apples, many more than the one from which the original seed came. These small things are considered by many of us as natural, but in reality, they are small miracles of God's creation. If you do not think they are miracles, then you start with nothing, make a seed, plant it, and try to grow a tree with a multitude of fruit. Man has yet to develop a machine that duplicates even once what God does everyday. Christ used these miracles time and time again in parables to teach us about God.

> *And he spake many things unto them in parables, saying, Behold, a sower went forth to sow; And when he sowed, some seeds fell by the way side, and the fowls came and devoured them up: Some fell upon stony places, where they had not much earth: and forthwith they sprung up, because they had no deepness of earth: And when the sun was up, they were scorched; and because they had no root, they withered away. And some fell among thorns; and the thorns sprung up, and choked them: But other fell into good ground, and brought forth fruit, some an hundredfold, some sixtyfold, some thirtyfold. Who hath ears to hear, let him hear. (Matthew 13:3-9)*

I Am Come To Bring Living Water

While Christ spoke of the miracle of planting and growing of seeds, the meaning to those that really hear and see in the Spirit (or are enlighten by Living Waters) is far more reaching. Since what happens with seeds is controlled by Laws of God, those same Laws apply to many other situations. Therefore he that has an ear for the things of God will hear the true meaning of the parable as it relates to Word of God as the seed and they that hear the Word of God as the ground in which the seed is planted.

Hear ye therefore the parable of the sower. When any one heareth the word of the kingdom, and understandeth it not, then cometh the wicked one, and catcheth away that which was sown in his heart. This is he which received seed by the way side. But he that received the seed into stony places, the same is he that heareth the word, and anon with joy receiveth it; Yet hath he not root in himself, but dureth for a while: for when tribulation or persecution ariseth because of the word, by and by he is offended. He also that received seed among the thorns is he that heareth the word; and the care of this world, and the deceitfulness of riches, choke the word, and he becometh unfruitful. But he that received seed into the good ground is he that heareth the word, and understandeth it; which also beareth fruit, and bringeth forth, some an hundredfold, some sixty, some thirty. (Matthew 13:18-23)

What is so interesting about the explanation of the parable is the ending in which we find people receive the seed (or hear the word of God) and understand it will bear fruit. That fruit will sometimes be thirty, sixty, and hundred fold. We also know the fruit must be after its own kind because that is the Law of God. So what is this fruit and how does the hearing and understanding of word result in fruit? I mean how does a seed turn into fruit?

Now I could discuss a lot of biology and show that each seed has within the seed the tiny embryo of the original plant along with necessary nutriment required to feed and fertilize the new plant when it decades and dies in the soil mixed with the right amount of water, but all that knowledge is available to you from the world. Instead I want to tell you the mystery of God working the miracle of the seed. You see, there is nothing man has been able to do that emulates the miracle God performs with every seed that grows into a plant. There are also no words in man's language that will explain what takes place. It is a miracle even if we all just think of it as an act of nature. If it was just an act of nature, then how did it start, when will it stop, and who is controlling it so it does not get out of hand. For example, if the miracle of a seed growing into a plant was totally random, then why does grass grow in some places and trees in others? If you say the seeds are just carried randomly by the wind or by birds, then why are the right-kinds of seeds that grow only certain climaxes always seem to be in the right places. I mean you do not find water lilies growing in the desert and you do not find desert plants growing by the sea and rivers. Who is controlling the order of things? Some of you may think it is all controlled by farmers that know how, where and when to plant. But consider how much a single man can learn. How many plants can you name and how many of them do you know where they grow? Unless you are the first Adam, I think you will fail the test before you name half the plants. Since the day Adam originally names them all, everyone else has failed to achieve the same level of knowledge. Keep in mind, the first Adam was without sin when he achieved that task.

Instead of the aforementioned paths of discussion that will only end in agreement to disagree concerning faith, I believe seeds in good soil multiplying in thirty, sixty, and hundred fold are the direct result of a miracles worked by God. All we need to do is have the faith to believe in the miracles. Some would say it is not faith in God, but faith in nature and therefore not a miracle. Well even if they are right, they still have to have faith the seed will multiply. It is the faith, no matter what the power behind it may be, that brings about the multiplication of the seeds into plants and fruit. Jesus put it this way.

And he said, So is the kingdom of God, as if a man should cast seed into the ground; And should sleep, and rise night and day, and the seed should spring and grow up, he knoweth not how. For the earth bringeth forth fruit of herself; first the blade, then the ear, after that the full corn in the ear. (Mark 4:26-28)

But the power that works in the earth to cause it to bring for the fruit is faith. It is just the reality of believing God will bring it to pass.

And Jesus said unto them, Because of your unbelief: for verily I say unto you, If ye have faith as a grain of mustard seed, ye shall say unto this mountain, Remove hence to yonder place; and it shall remove; and nothing shall be impossible unto you. Howbeit this kind goeth not out but by prayer and fasting. (Matthew 17:20-21)

A farmer plants a seed and anticipates it will grow. He comes back to the field after a few days and expects to see the plants growing. The farmer's confidence is just as sure as you are when you sit on a chair, the chair will hold you. Think about it, in most cases the chair weights less than you. So why is its strength great enough to hold you? Now physics would explain the strength based on the type of material and the structure of the chair. But aside from all that (some of which many of us will never understand), you and I still have the unyielding faith to believe the chair will hold us. In fact, we rarely look back at the chair as we recline. It sounds like a lot of trust or faith to me. In fact it sounds like the reality of believing the chair will hold us to me.

Consider how you jump up into the air sometimes. When you jump, you are confident gravity will pull you back down to the earth. If gravity did not do its job as we believe it would, we would just float off into space. But we are so sure of the reality of our belief in the effects of gravity, we do not even give it a second consideration. We just believe in the reality we will come back to earth if we jump up.

And that is the faith of a farmer that plants a seed. His faith is so sure, it is second nature. But regardless of what it is based on (God or nature), it is still faith. That is because having faith to believe the seed will grow does not require you to have faith to believe Jesus is the son of God. So you and I just come to accept

110

these things everyday. We just come to have the faith similar to that of a mustered seed about these things everyday. Well the things of the Lord are not any different. In fact they are the same and are controlled by the same Laws of God. That is why Jesus could use them (so called nature) time and time again to explain the things of God. God and his Laws do not change. They are the same yesterday, today, and forever. And God and his Laws are one. The same Law that applies to the seed, applies to the word, and applies to us.

So as a seed grows into a plant and bears fruit of its kind, so does the word of God in a Christian grows and bears fruit of its kind. So what is this fruit? It is an output resulting from the combination of the word of God (the seed) with Living Water (the Holy Spirit). The resulting fruit is after its kind.

And God said, Let us make man in our image, after our like-ness: and let them have dominion over the fish of the sea, and over the fowl of the air, and over the cattle, and over all the earth, and over every creeping thing that creepeth upon the earth. (Genesis 1:26)

Man is made in the image and likeness of God. God is a Spirit. Therefore man is made in the image and likeness of the Spirit of God. That is the kind of man. So the ouput that comes from the combination of the word of God (the seed) and the Liv-ing Water (the Holy Spirit) must be a Spiritual kind after the kind of man (the image of the Spiritual God). Paul stated it very sim-ply.

But the fruit of the Spirit is love, joy, peace, longsuffering, gentleness, goodness, faith, Meekness, temperance: against such there is no law. (Galatians 5:22-23)

To help understand the fruit of Living Water, let me first as Paul did, explain what is not the fruit of Living Water.

You know with the coming of Jesus and his sacrifice, we are no longer bond by a requirement to obey the law. In fact, the Law was removed from the old tablets of stone that were a burden to obey and is now written in our hearts. Jesus summed up all that is required to obey the law today.

Jesus said unto him, Thou shalt love the Lord thy God with all thy heart, and with all thy soul, and with all thy mind. This is the first and great commandment. And the second is like unto it, Thou shalt love thy neighbour as thyself. On these two commandments hang all the law and the prophets. (Matthew 22:37-40)

So if we love God and love neighbors as we love ourselves, then we would comply with the entirety of the Law.

For all the law is fulfilled in one word, even in this; Thou shalt love thy neighbour as thyself. (Galatians 5:14)

But we are no longer under the Law, but we are under the Spirit now. How then should we that are freed from the Law walk in Christ?

This I say then, Walk in the Spirit, and ye shall not fulfil the lust of the flesh. For the flesh lusteth against the Spirit, and the Spirit against the flesh: and these are contrary the one to the other: so that ye cannot do the things that ye would. But if ye be led of the Spirit, ye are not under the law. (Galatians 5:16-18)

As long as you walk in the Spirit (notice the capital "S") you cannot lust after the flesh. In other words, you cannot live in the flesh and the ways of the world if you are always in the way of Spirit. Once you got Living Water, you will not thirst, so you will never be tempted to drink the water of the world. It is the Law of God no one can serve two masters at once. Just like the same spring of water cannot bring forward both flesh water and sea (salt) water, you cannot have the fruit of the world and the fruit of God (or Living Water) coming out of you at the same time. The two are opposite. They fight each other and they will not occupy the same space in matter at the same time. If you still have not partook of the Living Waters, then every time you try to do right, wrong will be ever present in your mind trying to convince you to do wrong. You are still walking in the flesh giving opportunity to the things that are not of God. When you walk in the Spirit, the things of the world have no place in any part of your being and you will find it takes no special strength to do right because wrong is never present in your mind. Now being under the Spirit means you are free because you never think of the things of the world. All you want to do is please God. Since you are walking in the Spirit, there is nothing within the Spirit that does not want to continually please God.

It is like God standing before a mirror and seeing himself. The reflection is the Spirit of God. To become a part of that Spirit reflection, we must first become the same as that Spirit. We must become a perfect reflection of God. Man along cannot achieve that goal. But when we become part of the body of Christ, we can achieve that goal because Christ is the perfect reflection of God.

So what is not a part of the reflection of God? What is not the Spirit of God? What is not the fruit of the Spirit?

Now the works of the flesh are manifest, which are these; Adultery, fornication, uncleanness, lasciviousness, Idolatry, witchcraft, hatred, variance, emulations, wrath, strife, seditions, heresies, Envyings, murders, drunkenness, revellings, and such like: of the which I tell you before, as I have also told you in time past, that they which do such things shall not inherit the kingdom of God. (Galatians 5:19-21)

I am not going to explain these evil works of the flesh. I do not want to give them much attention. For if you think too much on these things, you will find them drawing you from the ways of God and peace you have available in God. However, I will provide you a brief set of definitions so you will understand each listed work of the flesh and be able to recognize if you are confronted by this evil. Please note this is a personal Word. It is not a Word to be used to judge others, but a Word to be used to personally judge you. Judge yourself and let God judge others.

I Am Come To Bring Living Water

Adultery
   Moicheia (Strong's Talking Greek & Hebrew Dictionary) –
"Conjugal infidelity. An adulterer was a man who had illicit intercourse with a married or a betrothed woman, and such a
woman was an adulteress. Intercourse between a married man
and an unmarried woman was fornication. Adultery was regarded
as a great social wrong, as well as a great sin." (Illustrated Bible
Dictionary: And Treasury of Biblical History, Biography, Geography, Doctrine, and Literature).

Fornication
   Porneia (Strong's Talking Greek & Hebrew Dictionary) –
This word is sometimes used to imply an adulterer. In addition,
"this word is more frequently used in a symbolical than in its ordinary sense. It frequently means a forsaking of God or a following after idols" (Illustrated Bible Dictionary: And Treasury of
Biblical History, Biography, Geography, Doctrine, and Literature).

Uncleanness
   Akatharsia - from (akathartos); *impurity* (the quality), physical or moral :- uncleanness (Strong's Talking Greek & Hebrew
Dictionary) - The distinctive idea attached to ceremonial uncleanness among the Hebrews was that it cut a person off for the
time from social privileges, and left his citizenship among God's
people for the while in abeyance. There is an intense reality in the
fact of the divine law taking hold of a man by the ordinary infirmities of flesh, and setting its stamp, as it were, in the lowest clay
of which he is moulded. The sacredness attached to the human
body is parallel to that which invested the ark of the covenant itself. It is as though Jehovah thereby would teach men that the
"very hairs of their head were all numbered" before him and that
"in his book were all their members written." Thus was incul-
cated so to speak a bodily holiness. Nor were the Israelites to be
only "separated from other people," but they were to be "holy to
God," Leviticus 20:24, 26 "a kingdom of priests, and a holy na-

tion." Smith's Bible Dictionary: Comprising Antiquities, Biography, Geography, Natural History, Archaeology and Literature.

Lasciviousness

Aselgeia - from a compound of (a) (as a negative particle) and a presumed selges (of uncertain derivative, but apparently meaning *continent*); *licentiousness* (sometimes including other vices):- filthy, lasciviousness, wantonness (Strong's Talking Greek & Hebrew Dictionary).

Idolatry

Eidōlolatria (Strong's Talking Greek & Hebrew Dictionary) - Image-worship or divine honour paid to any created object. Paul describes the origin of idolatry in Rom 1:21-25: men forsook God, and sank into ignorance and moral corruption (Rom 1:28). The forms of idolatry are,
(1.) Fetishism, or the worship of trees, rivers, hills, stones, etc.
(2.) Nature worship, the worship of the sun, moon, and stars, as the supposed powers of nature.
(3.) Hero worship, the worship of deceased ancestors, or of heroes.
(Illustrated Bible Dictionary: And Treasury of Biblical History, Biography, Geography, Doctrine, and Literature).

Witchcraft

Pharmakeia - from (pharmakeus); *medication* ("pharmacy"), i.e. (by extension) *magic* (literal or figurative):- sorcery, witchcraft (Strong's Talking Greek & Hebrew Dictionary) - In the popular sense of the word no mention is made either of witches or of witchcraft in Scripture. The "witch of En-dor" (1Sa 28) was a necromancer, i.e., one who feigned to hold converse with the dead. The damsel with "a spirit of divination" (Acts 16:16) was possessed by an evil spirit, or, as the words are literally rendered, "having a spirit, a pithon." The reference is to the heathen god Apollo, who was regarded as the god of prophecy. (Illustrated Bible Dictionary: And Treasury of Biblical History, Biography, Geography, Doctrine, and Literature).

I Am Come To Bring Living Water

Hatred
   Echthra - feminine of (echthros); *hostility*; by implication a reason for *opposition*:- enmity, hatred (Strong's Talking Greek & Hebrew Dictionary).

Variance
   Eris - of uncertain affinity; a *quarrel*, i.e. (by implication) *wrangling*: - contention, debate, strife, variance (Strong's Talking Greek & Hebrew Dictionary).

Emulations
   Zēlos - from (zeo); properly *heat*, i.e. (figurative) *"zeal"* (in a favorable sense, *ardor*; in an unfavorable one, *jealousy*, as of a husband [figurative of God], or an enemy, *malice*):- emulation, envy (-ing), fervent mind, indignation, jealousy, zeal (Strong's Talking Greek & Hebrew Dictionary).

Wrath
   Thymos - from (thuo); *passion* (as if *breathing* hard):- fierceness, indignation, wrath. Compare (psuche) (Strong's Talking Greek & Hebrew Dictionary).

Strife
   Eritheia - perhaps from the same as (erethizo); properly *intrigue*, i.e. (by implication) *faction* :- contention (-ious), strife (Strong's Talking Greek & Hebrew Dictionary).

Seditions
   Dichostasia - from a derivative of (dis) and (stasis); *disunion*, i.e. (figurative) *dissension* : - division, sedition (Strong's Talking Greek & Hebrew Dictionary).

Heresies
   Hairesis (Strong's Talking Greek & Hebrew Dictionary). - From a Greek word signifying (1) a choice, (2) the opinion chosen, and (3) the sect holding the opinion. In the Acts of the Apostles (Acts 5:17; Acts 15:5; Acts 24:5, 14; Acts 26:5) it denotes a sect, without reference to its character. Elsewhere, how-

ever, in the New Testament it has a different meaning attached to it. Paul ranks "heresies" with crimes and seditions (Gal 5:20). This word also denotes divisions or schisms in the church (1Co 11:19). In Tit 3:10 a "heretical person" is one who follows his own self-willed "questions," and who is to be avoided. Heresies thus came to signify self-chosen doctrines not emanating from God (2Pe 2:1) (Illustrated Bible Dictionary: And Treasury of Biblical History, Biography, Geography, Doctrine, and Literature).

Envyings

Phthonos - probably akin to the base of (phtheiro); *ill-will* (as *detraction*), i.e. *jealousy* (*spite*):- envy (Strong's Talking Greek & Hebrew Dictionary).

Murders

Phonos (Strong's Talking Greek & Hebrew Dictionary) - Willful murder was distinguished from accidental homicide, and was invariably visited with capital punishment (Num 35:16, 18, 21, 31; Lev 24:17). This law in its principle is founded on the fact of man's having been made in the likeness of God (Gen 9:5, 6; John 8:44; 1Jn 3:12, 15). The Mosiac law prohibited any compensation for murder or the reprieve of the murderer (Ex 21:12, 14; Deut 19:11, 13; 2Sa 17:25; 2Sa 20:10). Two witnesses were required in any capital case (Num 35:19-30; Deut 17:6-12). If the murderer could not be discovered, the city nearest the scene of the murder was required to make expiation for the crime committed (Deut 21:1-9). These offences also were to be punished with death, (1) striking a parent; (2) cursing a parent; (3) kidnapping (Ex 21:15-17; Deut 27:16) (Illustrated Bible Dictionary: And Treasury of Biblical History, Biography, Geography, Doctrine, and Literature).

Drunkenness

Methē (Strong's Talking Greek & Hebrew Dictionary). - The first case of intoxication on record is that of Noah (Gen 9:21). The sin of drunkenness is frequently and strongly condemned (Rom 13:13; 1Co 6:9, 10; Eph 5:18; 1Th 5:7, 8). The sin of drinking to excess seems to have been not uncommon among the Israelites. The word is used figuratively, when men are spoken of as being drunk with sorrow, and with the wine of God's wrath (Isa 63:6; Jer 51:57; Ezek 23:33). To "add drunkenness to thirst" ((Deut 29:19), A.V.) is a proverbial expression, rendered in the Revised Version "to destroy the moist with the dry", i.e., the well-watered equally with the dry land, meaning that the effect of such walking in the imagination of their own hearts would be to destroy one and all (Illustrated Bible Dictionary: And Treasury of Biblical History, Biography, Geography, Doctrine, and Literature).

Revellings
    Kōmos - from (keimai); a *carousal* (as if a *letting loose*) :- revelling, rioting (Strong's Talking Greek & Hebrew Dictionary).

But the fruit of the Spirit is love, joy, peace, longsuffering, gentleness, goodness, faith, Meekness, temperance: against such there is no law. (Galatians 5:22-23)

Love is the first and most important fruit of the Spirit. A saint that is full of Living Water (the Spirit of God) is also full of love. I could try to explain this love by providing the definitions of the four words in Greek used for love and explain this love as agape, but that would not provide you with an image of love. I could as many others have presented John 3:16 and explain love by showing you the love God has for us, but that would not provide you with an image of love. Instead let me explain God's plan for you and me. You see God loves us so much he has since the time he formed Adam out of the earth and he disobeyed, been trying to bring us to a position where we can join him (become one in Christ and one in God) and enter into his rest. God is at rest, his work was completed at the end of day six and he has been at rest since that day awaiting our arrival. Our imperfections prevent our entrance into that rest of God. Christ is already there and he also awaits our arrival. After all these years in the eyes of man, he is still waiting our arrival. Now that is true love, a love that does not give up even when he knows our imperfec-

tions (our sins). Consider how God has shown his love over time
and realized he only wanted or wants today is we love him as he
has loved us and we love our brothers and sisters with the same
love.

When Adam and Eve committed the first sin, God did not destroy them. No he loved them so much he provided an opportunity by grace to return to his favor. It did not seem so at the time,
but being put out of the Garden of Eden and made to till the soil
and suffer in child birth was an act of grace. The punishment or
the payment for sin is death and God loved them so much he let
them live. He showed the same love when he allow Noah and his
family to live while he destroyed all other men and women.
Then he empowered them to build man's race again. God loved
and chose Abram and decided to make his offspring his chosen
people. Over the many years since, with all the ups and downs of
the relationship such as living as a rich and successful people for
three glorious generations in the beginning, living in Egypt and
falling into slavery, escaping to the wilderness, wondering forty
years, going to the promise land and being put back into captivity
several times and even the struggles and wars associated with Israel today, all God really wanted or wants is for Israel to love him
as he has loved them and Israel to love their brothers and sisters
with the same love.

Then God sent his only son. He gave the ultimate gift of
love. The Father gave his own son and that son gave his life. It
was done out of love. Israel rejected the son and he went to other
nations with the same love. And all God wanted or wants today
is we love him as he has loved us and we love our brothers and
sisters with the same love.

There is an ancient story in one of the lost books of the bible
(The Hymn of the Pearl) found with the old scrolls about the re-
trieval of a pearl. The parents sent their youngest son to a far
away land to retrieve a very rare lost pearl. The young child had
to take off all his garments that were made for him in his Father's
palace and put on the garments of the people in the land (Egypt)
that was far away from his palace home. He wanted to be able to
move among the people and accomplish his goal without being
detected by those that would defeat his purpose. The pearl was

119

kept by a serpent and the young child wanted to wait until the serpent slept before he tried to take the pearl. Yet when the young child came to the land far from his home and began to associate with the people he made a close comrade of one fair and beautiful youth that was the son of a courtier. The young child began eating and drinking with the people of Egypt and soon forgot his mission. The young child could no longer remember he was the son of a King and fell into a very deep sleep. Before long he no longer remembered where he was from or his need to complete the mission and return home. Then his father the King, his mother and brother decided he should not be left loss in Egypt, so they sent him a letter. The letter said awake from your sleep and remember your princely garments and the kingdom you will one day share with your brother. When the young child read the letter, he was awakened and remembered his mission. He at once snatched the pearl and returned to his parents. As he journeyed home, he stripped of the dirty Egyptian clothing and put back on his royal silken garments that were made for him in his Father's palace. Dressed in those garments with the pearl in hand he entered the doors of the King to appear before the King while all the subjects sang hymns with harmonious voices.

I think you can easily see the similarity of the ancient story and the story of Christ. In my view, the pearl is the Living Waters (the Holy Spirit) that is hidden inside of you and me and has been since the day God put the breath of life (his Spirit) in Adam. But that pearl is lost and in need of a guide to get home. So God the Father sent his only son into a far away place to retrieve the pearl inside of us. His son Christ put on the garment of mankind. He was born of man and lived amongst us. And I am thankful, as he grew up as a child, he did not forget the mission of his Father. He did not fall into a deep sleep, but instead he grew up, left his earthly father and mother and went about to do the will of his heavenly Father. He was the Word. He was the letter sent from the Father to awaken us. He taught and preached that letter or that Word to us to awaken the pearl inside of us and make us realize our need to go home to the Father. And we that heard that Word while he walked this earth and afterwards from his disciples, apostles, teachers, and witnessing saints, were awaken and we now work in the vineyard of wining other brothers and sisters for the Lord and awaiting the homecoming and the true rest in the Lord. When that day comes, we too will put on a royal robe and enter into the doors of the King with our pearl, the gift of the Holy Spirit. Now that is true Love of the Father for the children, love of the child for the Father, and love for our brothers and sisters. And all God wanted or wants today is we love him as he has loved us and we love our brothers and sisters with the same love.

A saint that is full of Living Waters (the Holy Spirit) is also full of the fruit called **joy**. Joy is "Chara" in the Greek and it means great gladness, cheerfulness, delight, and fullness. Now joy is a fruit of reaction. If you have joy, there should also be a reason for the joy. Maybe you have seen people that smile all the time. They do not smile because they are happy, but they smile because they are trying to make a certain impression. They are trying to impress people into believing they have joy. Well that is not the joy I am explaining here. The joy I am explaining is a reactionary. Just think of what God has done for you. You do not have to think too long. Don't just concentrate on the big things, but think of the little things. Just think, you got up this morning and found the bed you were lying in did not become your death bed. You say God does that everyday. Yes he does, but how often do you stop to thank him for doing it everyday. You just take it for granted, but it is much more than a small thing. To get out of bed, your heart had to change its rate; parts of your body that had been temporally paralyzed to keep you from walking away in your sleep, now had to be un-paralyzed. Your eyes had to open. Blood circulation had to increase. Nerves, which were inactive, became active. Your senses that had been turned off in the night had to come back to life so you could see the room around you, feel the floor under your feet, smell and taste the steal mouth that results from a night of limited use. It is at a time like that I think of how much God does for me even without my asking. I think of how wonderful he protected me all night. I may not know what the day will bring. I may not have all I think I need to live another day. I may be facing this day greater trails than I think I can bear. I may think I am all along. I may be trouble by too many others depending on me. I may wish to go back to bed and just not face my day. But one thing is for sure. I am still here another day and God is the reason I am still here. It is at a time like that I just cry out loudly, "Thank you Jesus". And the joy that floods my soul is more than I can contain. I began to praise God. I have to pray. I have to thank God for what he has done for me, the big things and the small things. I just start listing not what I want him to do, but what he has already done. That's why I have joy. That is the joy the world did not give to me. It is a joy in reaction to the goodness of God in my life. It is a great gladness I cannot contain, so I let it out in the form of praises. The scriptures teach God resides in the praises of his people.

But thou art holy, O thou that inhabitest the praises of Israel. (Psalm 22:3)

And scriptures teach the joy of the Lord is your strength.

Then he said unto them, Go your way, eat the fat, and drink the sweet, and send portions unto them for whom nothing is prepared: for this day is holy unto our Lord: neither be ye sorry; for the joy of the LORD is your strength. (Nehemiah 8:10)

So if you are missing the joy I speak about, perhaps you are trying to have joy that is not reactionary. You have to have a reason for joy. Start to think of what God has done for you and it will not be long before the joy comes. And it will not be a fake thing you use to impress others. It will be an internal joy based on what God has done for you.

There is one more comment I need to make about joy. Earlier in this book, I discussed the references in the scriptures on Living Water. There is one more reference I have not discussed. It is found in the book of Revelation. It is the ultimate reason for my joy. All my reactions for the little things God has done are nothing in comparison to the greatest thing God shall do and has already performed the work to do for me. You see our entire walk in this world is designed for one purpose only. I know this may sound strange to those that teach you need to find your purpose in life. Well I have search and I have found one and only one purpose. That purpose is the same for all true saints of God. It is the reason God first spoke to Abram and led him to a land of promise. It is the reason God kept the promise to Abram with his son Isaac and his son Jacob. It is the reason Joseph was saved from death in prison and Moses saved so many from bondage. It is the reason David praised the Lord and the reason God spoke with the prophets of old. It is the reason Jesus came into this world and die for us.

And after these things I saw four angels standing on the four corners of the earth, holding the four winds of the earth, that the wind should not blow on the earth, nor on the sea, nor on any tree. And I saw another angel ascending from the east, having the seal of the living God: and he cried with a loud voice to the four angels, to whom it was given to hurt the earth and the sea, Saying, Hurt not the earth, neither the sea, nor the trees, till we have sealed the servants of our God in their foreheads. And I heard the number of them which were sealed: and there were sealed an hundred and forty and four thousand of all the tribes of the children of Israel. Of the tribe of Juda were sealed twelve thousand. Of the tribe of Reuben were sealed twelve thousand. Of the tribe of Gad were sealed twelve thousand. Of the tribe of Aser were sealed twelve thousand. Of the tribe of Nepthalim were sealed twelve thousand. Of the tribe of Manasses were sealed twelve thousand. Of the tribe of Simeon were sealed twelve thousand. Of the tribe of Levi were sealed twelve thousand. Of the tribe of Issachar were sealed twelve thousand. Of the tribe of Zabulon were sealed twelve thousand. Of the tribe of Joseph were sealed twelve thousand. Of the tribe of Benjamin were sealed twelve thousand. After this I beheld, and, lo, a great multitude, which no man could number, of all nations, and kindreds, and people, and tongues, stood before the throne, and before the Lamb, clothed with white robes, and palms in their hands; And cried with a loud voice, saying, Salvation to our God which sitteth upon the throne, and unto the Lamb. And

I Am Come To Bring Living Water

all the angels stood round about the throne, and about the elders and the four beasts, and fell before the throne on their faces, and worshipped God, Saying, Amen: Blessing, and glory, and wisdom, and thanksgiving, and honour, and power, and might, be unto our God for ever and ever. Amen. And one of the elders answered, saying unto me, What are these which are arrayed in white robes? and whence came they? And I said unto him, Sir, thou knowest. And he said to me, These are they which came out of great tribulation, and have washed their robes, and made them white in the blood of the Lamb. Therefore are they before the throne of God, and serve him day and night in his temple: and he that sitteth on the throne shall dwell among them. They shall hunger no more, neither thirst any more; neither shall the sun light on them, nor any heat. For the Lamb which is in the midst of the throne shall feed them, and shall lead them unto living fountains of waters: and God shall wipe away all tears from their eyes. (Revelation 7:1-17)

You see this joy I have is because I know I will be in the number that stand before God. I know I will wear a white robe that has been washed in the blood of the Lamb of God. I know I will be there to offer praise and sing a song the angels cannot sing because they have not lived the tribulation I have lived. I know my trails and tribulation will be over. I know I will not hunger, thirst, or suffer anymore. I will be fed by the Lamb and my thirst will be fulfilled by the fountains of Living Waters. I will be immersed in the fountains. I will be immersed in the Spirit of God and God himself will wipe away all my tears. That is why this joy I have; the world did not give it to me. This is my purpose in life and this is your purpose in life. Anything short of this purpose, no mater how good it may seem is not eternal and will also pass away.

Just like the two aforementioned fruits, **Peace** (eirēnē) is also directly related to God's actions in our lives. Maybe you missed that point. Love is a fruit of the Living Water in me because it is an emulation of God's love for me demonstrated by his plan for my salvation. Joy is a fruit of Living Water in me because it is my personal reaction to all God has done for me. Peace similarly is a fruit of the Living Water in me because it is a rest of my will and an acceptance of God's will. Oh, you may have never heard anyone explain peace that way.

The only time I am anxious, worried, troubled, disturbed, tried, etc. is when I am responsible and things are dependent on my actions. But when I am not responsible, when no one including myself are dependent on me, or when I have no care of what the outcome may be, I am the most happy and the most at peace. It is a time such as that I can find rest from my works and truly experience quietness. There are some great scriptures in the bible that explain peace, but let me tell you what an old saint said to me about one such text.

This dear sister in the Lord was caring for a young child given to her guardianship in old age. One day that young child (about 5 years old at the time) was hit by a car. At the hospital, the dear sister was told, he broke almost every bone in his body. He was in a coma and anticipated to die soon. This dear sister went into an empty room at the hospital and started talking to the only physician she trusted. She was worried. She did not know what to do for her child. She desired to do something. She was in prayer asking God what she could do. She had no peace.

God spoke to her heart and directed her to open the bible to Philippians 4:4 and she read

Rejoice in the Lord alway: and again I say, Rejoice. Let your moderation be known unto all men. The Lord is at hand. (Philippians 4:4-5)

She began to rejoice. Even with her child close to death, she rejoiced because the Lord said to rejoice. She began to express the child was in the Lord's hand and he was able to heal the child. She let the world know the Lord was at that hospital and he was in charge of the child's care. She showed her moderation, meaning her gentle patients. Then she read

Be careful for nothing; but in every thing by prayer and supplication with thanksgiving let your requests be made known

unto God. And the peace of God, which passeth all under-
standing, shall keep your hearts and minds through Christ Je-
sus. (Philippians 4:6-7)

So she did. She told the Lord what she wanted. She asked
the Lord to heal her child and not to take the child from her.
Once she gave this problem to the Lord, she had peace. She did
not have any need left to worry. It was no longer her responsibility. The Lord had taken over giving her a peace which passed all
understanding. It was peaceful because she kept her mind on Jesus and not on her problem.

God healed the child. When I was introduced to the child, he
was eighteen years old. He walked with a little limp, but otherwise, you could not tell he had ever been in an accident. In fact,
when the dear sister told me the story, I initially assumed she was
talking about a child different from the young man she introduced. Your concern may be different from the dear sister. Your
concern may not involve a healing. Your concern may just be a
sin or a temptation to sin. You may just be struggling with how
to keep yourself in obedience of the Lord with all the temptations
we face from day to day. One day I asked God how I can overcome temptation and the sins that come so easy when we yield to
the temptations. Yes, I struggle just like everybody else. God
gave me an answer and it was the next scripture in Philippians.

Finally, brethren, whatsoever things are true, whatsoever
things are honest, whatsoever things are just, whatsoever
things are pure, whatsoever things are lovely, whatsoever
things are of good report; if there be any virtue, and if there
be any praise, think on these things. Those things, which ye
have both learned, and received, and heard, and seen in me,
do: and the God of peace shall be with you. (Philippians 4:8-
9)

If I spend all my time thinking on true, honest, just, pure, and
lovely things and things of good report, I will not have time to
think on things that are not of God. I will not be tempted because
I will not give an ear to any source of temptation. And if I also

only do the things I have learned, received, heard and seen in Christ, I will have peace, even peace from all my temptations and sins!

The only time I am anxious, worried, troubled, disturbed, tried, etc. is when I am responsible and things are dependent on my actions. But when I am not responsible, when no one including myself are dependent on me, or when I have no care of what the outcome may be, I am the most happy and the most at peace. It is a time such as that I can find rest from my works and truly experience quietness. I then enter true rest of my will and an acceptance of God's will, which is peace.

Longsuffering (makrothymia) referring to fortitude and patience to forebear is a fruit of the Living Water that goes hand and hand with peace. Because when you have the peace to put it all into God's hands, it is the same faith that will guide you to leave burdens and worries in God's hands. Don't go back and claim them.

Many bible students explaining longsuffering will speak on patience and the willingness of Saints to endure suffering for a long time. They use examples of people that can somehow stand or put up with forms of abuse (physical, mental, or spiritual) for long periods of time and remain humble and non retaliatory. And I do not disagree with those views. I think those teachings have their need in the body of Christ. But I also think those teaching lean more to the worldly definition of longsuffering than to the spiritual definition. The worldly definitions are as an adjective – bearing injury, insults, trouble, etc. patiently for a long time and as a noun – long and patient endurance of injuries, insults, trouble, etc. But I do not know how to achieve those attributes that define the word longsuffering without the power of God.

I think what must take place is you must become unburdened of the things you will long suffer. It is like the ancient Jewish believer taking his sins to the Tabernacle or the Temple and allowing the Priest to transfer those sins two goats. One goat to be put to death at the alter as a blood offering to God to purge the sins away and another to be the scapegoat to take those sins away from the camp and the people. Then the Jew that had the sin is able to suffer long knowing he had previously committed the sin because it has been removed from him and the camp. The weight has been lifted. God has forgotten the sin so the Jew no longer fears death from the sin. The Jew never had the strength to endure it before, but now that God has taken it away, he can endure.

> *And he shall take of the congregation of the children of Israel two kids of the goats for a sin offering, and one ram for a burnt offering. And Aaron shall offer his bullock of the sin offering, which is for himself, and make an atonement for himself, and for his house. And he shall take the two goats, and present them before the LORD at the door of the tabernacle of the congregation. And Aaron shall cast lots upon the two goats; one lot for the LORD, and the other lot for the scapegoat. And Aaron shall bring the goat upon which the LORD'S lot fell, and offer him for a sin offering. But the goat, on which the lot fell to be the scapegoat, shall be presented alive before the LORD, to make an atonement with him, and to let him go for a scapegoat into the wilderness. (Leviticus 16:5-10)*

I know that may sounds strange to some as a way to define longsuffering. But I think the right definition of the fruit of Living Water has to also provide a means of obtaining the fruit. On my own, I am not able to suffer very long. When a boss at work persecutes me, others at Church disrespect me, a family member continually belittle and abuse me, or when children disobey me out of disrespect, I am not able to bear these burdens along. I am not physically able to suffer those things very long. Most of us have in our self a will that says that is enough and I cannot take anymore. But we that are in Christ have learned the Christ that is within us can take a lot more. It is this Christ in the form of Living Water or the Spirit of God that is able to make us hold our peace under stress. It makes us able to bear the burden and to suffer a little longer. And why is it possible, because we are not carrying the load. We gave the load to another. Just like the Jew that took his sins to the altar, we took our burdens to Christ and we left them there. So there is no longer a load to bear. You suffer for a long time, because you are not suffering, but he that is within you is suffering for you.

So put your troubles in God's hand and leave them there. One of the hardest things to do is simply to trust God. Once you have given your burden to God, do not try to pick it up again. Put it out of your thinking, out of your actions, and out of your consideration. Do not think of the burden or possible solutions to the problem. Do not even go back to God continually checking to see what he did. Just trust God. And that is the key to long-suffering. It does not take God sent lessons in patience as many may have previously taught; it just takes trust in God. I for one believe if Job had fully trusted God, then his suffering as the devil tried him would have been much shorter because the devil would have been putting God to the test rather than Job.

Gentleness (chrēstotēs) is one of personal critical fruits of Living Water. Critical because it is one of the personal fruits that will be felt first by those around you that potentially shall be drawn to Christ.

Two things are being explained at the same time. Sometimes we get so caught up in the power of Living Water (the Holy Spirit) we forget the primary purpose. When Jesus promised the coming of the Holy Spirit, he also gave the purpose of its coming. While it is easy to get carried away with the gifts and fruit, we should never loose site of the purpose.

But ye shall receive power, after that the Holy Ghost is come upon you: and ye shall be witnesses unto me both in Jerusalem, and in all Judaea, and in Samaria, and unto the uttermost part of the earth. (Acts 1:8)

Clearly in Acts, Jesus proclaims the power of the Holy Ghost for the purpose of being enabled to witness unto me (Christ) in Jerusalem, Judaea, Samaria, and the uttermost part of the earth. This power is given to make us witness. This power is given to allow us to spread the Gospel and win believers unto Christ. And just to make it easier. You do not have to worry about speaking to strangers about Jesus when you witness. There is no need for that kind of fear. Because he said witness unto me, meaning

I Am Come To Bring Living Water

Christ. Every time you tell somebody about Jesus, you should not think you are speaking to those persons. You should think you are speaking to Jesus. When a preacher or teacher preach and teach, they are not speaking to an audience, they are speaking to Jesus. There should be no fear of being in front of people because you are just in front of Jesus. The people around you just happen to be listening in on your conversation with Christ.

So the power of the Holy Ghost is for the purpose of witnessing. And the fruit of the Spirit are attributes given to the witness to enhance acceptance. That is why gentleness is so critical. Gentleness is one of the first things others will sense (whether physically via our six senses or spiritually) when meeting you. Let me give you an example of how the world has twisted this gift into something that is not of the Lord to show you what is of the Lord. I was taught in a college Business School how to make initial impressions on people when I first meet them. That impression is very critical because in many cases it will formulate how those people envision you for the remainder of your relationship. I learned all the tricks. You know like making sure someone the other person trusts build you up by boasting about you prior to the meeting. I was taught to walk in with confidence and my head held high with a serious small smile (no teeth) on my face. Most of all I was taught to grasp the person with a strong tight firm hand shake. Now all of that is almost the complete opposite of the fruit of the Spirit. Maybe I could say my business school training did not negate the fruit of love, joy, peace or longsuffering. But starting with the fruit of gentleness, things get a little personal and maybe negated by my business school training. It is a switch from having God's or Christ attributes inside of me to having a truly changed image of my own that results from having Christ inside of me. If I walk up to you and grasp your hand with a strong tight firm hand shake, then the one thing you will not sense (physically or spiritually) is gentleness. I hope you see how the world turns good to evil with such a simple training the world thinks makes a lot of sense. Relax you hand, come across as gentle (morally excellent character and demeanor with real kindness). It does not make you weak or soft. It makes you gentle.

I Am Come To Bring Living Water

Consider a lily in the field, it looks gentle. You can easily walk up and push it in any direction you want. You can even pull it out of the ground with little to no strength. But that same lily is able to withstand some of the strongest winds and rain storms God can send and live. Gentleness is not a sign of weakness.

It is this gentleness that will draw others to the Christ that is within you. This gentleness will entreat them and make them want to know more about you. They will notice the difference and not be able to put a finger on why you are different. But most important, they will want to know why. I use to sit in business meetings with a room full of people I did not know and make only one or two comments that were so full of the Holy Ghost fruits half the room came to me at break time to try to get to know what kind of man I am. It is not I was great, it was just I knew how to show my fruit. And those were business meetings that never discussed Christ. Just think how much more of a draw I could be if I were witnessing to Christ in front of the same people.

Notice this fruit is personal. Gentleness is not Christ inside of me being seen as gentle. No, this time it is me being gentle because Christ has changed me.

The same is true with the fruit of Living Water called **goodness** (agathōsynē), a virtue of beneficence. Goodness is also not Christ within me, but something I have become because Christ changed me.

> *And when he was gone forth into the way, there came one running, and kneeled to him, and asked him, Good Master, what shall I do that I may inherit eternal life? And Jesus said unto him, Why callest thou me good? there is none good but one, that is, God. (Mark 10:17-18)*

There is no way we can become good. Even Christ said the only one that is good is God. So being Christ like will not make be good. But this Spiritual fruit is not good, it is goodness. I may not be able to become good, but I can display the things that are good or in other words goodness. I can display acts of goodness that will seem like the good that is God's along. I can act like the image of God that I am and show goodness. This then becomes my personal virtue. This fruit is displayed in my daily actions. Goodness is not measured by how someone looks or sounds, but instead by the actions someone performs. It is my job to do that which is good, not for myself, but for others. If I only do good things for myself, I am not displaying a fruit of the Spirit, but a sin of selfishness in my life. Therefore, let us be good to others to the same degree we would want someone to do good for us. Then we are displaying goodness.

To do good things, you must have the opportunity. That is very easy to obtain, for needs are constantly around us. The problem becomes will you recognize the needs, when you are confronted?

For I was an hungred, and ye gave me meat: I was thirsty, and ye gave me drink: I was a stranger, and ye took me in: Naked, and ye clothed me: I was sick, and ye visited me: I was in prison, and ye came unto me. Then shall the righteous answer him, saying, Lord, when saw we thee an hungred, and fed thee? or thirsty, and gave thee drink? When saw we thee a stranger, and took thee in? or naked, and clothed thee? Or when saw we thee sick, or in prison, and came unto thee? And the King shall answer and say unto them, Verily I say unto you, Inasmuch as ye have done it unto one of the least of these my brethren, ye have done it unto me. Then shall he say also unto them on the left hand, Depart from me, ye cursed, into everlasting fire, prepared for the devil and his angels: For I was an hungred, and ye gave me no meat: I was thirsty, and ye gave me no drink: I was a stranger, and ye took me not in: naked, and ye clothed me not: sick, and in prison, and ye visited me not. Then shall they also answer him, saying, Lord, when saw we thee an hungred, or athirst, or a stranger, or naked, or sick, or in prison, and did not minister unto thee? Then shall he answer them, saying, Verily I say unto you, Inasmuch as ye did it not to one of the least of these, ye did it not to me. (Matthew 25:35-45)

I Am Come To Bring Living Water

The opportunity is all around you. It comes from all that are in need. If you stop to evaluated or judge the need to determine if it is real or not, then you will miss the opportunity to do goodness. You see, it is not my job to judge the needs of others. If I judge their needs, then I am a judge and not one that obeys the Lord. But we all know God is the only judge. Just take the time to think over the last whole day you were allowed to enjoy. Think of everyone you came to contact. Did you see, think, or hear of the sick, hungry, thirsty, stranger in your area, the poorly clothed, or the prisoner? Did you minister to them? Did you help them or those that were concerned for them? Did you even pray for them? Now notice, you do not have to evaluate their needs. That is not your job in displaying your fruit. You do not have to ask if they are part of the body of Christ. That is also not your job in displaying your fruit. Your job is to do goodness. The rest belongs to God. I know some of you are thinking about the scriptures related to letting your good be spoken of as evil.

Let not then your good be evil spoken of: (Romans 14:16)

I experienced the true context of this scripture. Once while I was running the center for the transcendent, a young man who was a Hare Krishna needed a place to sleep and was directed to the center by local police. We were full the night he arrived, but I like to do all I can to not turn anyone away. Now I knew he was Hare Krishna and therefore not of the body of Christ, but that did not matter. It was not my job to judge him. I did not have an extra bed, but I gave him space on the floor with bedding materials. I offered to share my own bed with the young man, but he declined as I expected due to his religious beliefs. The next day, I gave him a ride to the expressway as he requested. His plan was to hitch hike from Florida to New York. I could only pray for his success. Now on the way to the expressway, I asked if he was hungry. He said yes. I stopped at a fast food restaurant and purchase a breakfast for him. I gave it to him and he told me he could not eat the food because it was against his religious practices. Now the food I offered was all I had and he refused the food. Rather than letting my good become evil spoken of because if accepted it would cause the young man to sin in his religion, I instead asked him to keep the food and to offer it to some other hungry person waiting for a ride at the expressway. He smile and said, "You are doing a good deed". The scripture in Romans is not an instruction to judge the people you are helping to assure they are worthy. It is an instruction to not cause someone to sin because of your goodness. When I told the Hare Krishna to give the food to someone else in need, I was still feeding the hungry and in this case I will never know who received that blessing. In fact, I was also enabling the Hare Krishna to do good by feeding the hungry. Do "good" for others at every opportunity and you will display the fruit of goodness.

Faith (pistis) is a fruit I could write an entire book about. In fact I could write several books. Many others have already done so. I am not going to try to write something here that will by any means equal those that are bless of God to be teachers on Faith. I recommend your study of their teachings. Faith is not just a fruit. It is also a tool we Christians need to be able to live in this world on our way home. The definition of faith in this passage is assurance, belief, believe, and fidelity. Now please do not accept this as the complete definition of faith, there are many other scriptures to consider when defining the word. But this definition does indicate something I will explain about faith.

Faith is for a purpose. Many of us are aware of its purposes for this life. Some know how to operate in the laws of faith. Some know how to apply faith to obtain the things God has already provided for us. But did you know there is an ultimate purpose for faith? And did you know that ultimate purpose is to grant rest?

Let us therefore fear, lest, a promise being left us of entering into his rest, any of you should seem to come short of it. For unto us was the gospel preached, as well as unto them: but the word preached did not profit them, not being mixed with faith in them that heard it. For we which have believed do enter into rest, as he said, As I have sworn in my wrath, if they shall enter into my rest: although the works were finished from the foundation of the world. For he spake in a certain place of the seventh day on this wise, And God did rest the seventh day from all his works. And in this place again, If they shall enter into my rest. Seeing therefore it remaineth that some must enter therein, and they to whom it was first preached entered not in because of unbelief: Again, he lim- iteth a certain day, saying in David, To day, after so long a time; as it is said, To day if ye will hear his voice, harden not your hearts. For if Jesus had given them rest, then would he not afterward have spoken of another day. There remaineth therefore a rest to the people of God. For he that is entered into his rest, he also hath ceased from his own works, as God did from his. Let us labour therefore to enter into that rest, lest any man fall after the same example of unbelief. For the word of God is quick, and powerful, and sharper than any twoedged sword, piercing even to the dividing asunder of soul and spirit, and of the joints and marrow, and is a discerner of the thoughts and intents of the heart. Neither is there any creature that is not manifest in his sight: but all things are naked and opened unto the eyes of him with whom we have to do. Seeing then that we have a great high priest, that is passed into the heavens, Jesus the Son of God, let us hold fast our profession. For we have not an high priest which cannot be touched with the feeling of our infirmities; but was in all points tempted like as we are, yet without sin. Let us therefore come boldly unto the throne of grace, that we may obtain mercy, and find grace to help in time of need. (Hebrews 4:1- 16)

The book of Hebrews is often referred to explain the meaning of faith, but most go to the eleventh chapter that opens with the definition of faith and continues with several examples of faith. But let us not loose sight of the reason the Hebrew writer in- cluded this chapter. He wanted us to understand what faith is re- quired to enter into the rest of the Lord. While the definition given works miracles everyday for so many believers, it is also designed to work the ultimate miracle and that miracle being our key to enter into the rest of the Lord. Rethinking the eleventh chapter with this in mind will give you new insight about the specific examples of faith selected.

This is plainly stated in the fourth chapter. We are working toward the promise of rest. That is the purpose of the hearing of the gospel. Not all will hear and believe, but we that seek the rest have the faith to believe we will achieve it. The means of achieving the rest were put into place from the time of the foundations of the world. That is why God rested on the seven day after forming the world. And he has been resting every since, waiting on us to enter into the rest with him. I know you image God sitting waiting on our every prayer and responding with the miracles that grace our lives. But in reality, he knew those needs before he completed the foundations of the world and he has already answered those prayers even before we knew we had the need. That is why faith works. He has already done it. So believing becomes easy. You do not believe in something he will do, but rather something he has already done.

Some think they have already obtained the rest by just accepting Jesus. But if that was all there will be, then why did Jesus tell us of the promise? Why did he say?

Let not your heart be troubled: ye believe in God, believe also in me. In my Father's house are many mansions: if it were not so, I would have told you. I go to prepare a place for you. And if I go and prepare a place for you, I will come again, and receive you unto myself; that where I am, there ye may be also. And whither I go ye know, and the way ye know. (John 14:1-4)

It was because there is still a rest to come. A rest greater than any rest we have known to date. You know when you pray for God's assistance, you are generally in trouble and have exhausted all your capability. Now when God answers that prayer and bless you, you are happy and full of joy. All at once the burden is easier. But image what it would be like to not just have the burden made lighter, but to have the burden eliminated. In fact what would it be like to have the cause and the maker of the burden eliminated for ever. That is the true rest. You will never have to be burdened again because there is no such thing as burdens with the Lord in the Kingdom of Heaven. You will never be in need again because there is no need in Christ in the Kingdom of Heaven. You will never desire again because his rest is the fulfillment of all your hearts desires. There will be nothing that stands in the way of your praising God. There will be nothing to tempt you, nothing to trouble you, nothing to draw your thinking away from God. That is rest. That is the true rest in the Lord.

We labor to get to this rest. The word of God is refining us day by day like iron sharpening iron, like the potter molding clay, and like the silversmith polishing silver in preparation of this rest. The work of God is doing it full work inside of us that we will be presented to God pure and ready for this rest.

So this is the faith we have as a fruit of the Living Water. This faith that is not just to do the small things of working miracles here on earth. It is a faith that is more than just a tool to heal us, finance us, strengthen us, or unburden us. It is a faith that will take us home and present us to God so we may enter into the true rest in the Lord. I do not want to seem to belittle the great teachings of others about faith, but I do want to share with you the ultimate goal of our faith and that being the strength and tool required for following Christ our High Priest and entering into the rest of the Lord.

A saint fill with Living Water will have **meekness** (praotēs) meaning a very gentle humility. This fruit is also personal. It is a virtue of the saint and not the Christ within the saint. It is the result of being changed by Christ.

Humility is a virtue that only occurs as you accept a servant's character, even if you are the leader. For example, several saints attempt to be humble by being quiet and timid. But real humility is more. James warns us of our faith (belief) without our works. Anytime we have to profess our belief rather than demonstrate our belief, then we are showing faith without works.

Who is a wise man and endued with knowledge among you? let him shew out of a good conversation his works with meekness of wisdom. (James 3:13)

I Am Come To Bring Living Water

James was trying to get us to learn to be humble.

Humble yourselves in the sight of the Lord, and he shall lift you up. (James 4:10)

Let me try to make sense of these passages about being meek. Meekness is not just being timid. It is taking on a different attitude because you assume a different station in life. We all envision ourselves in various levels of maturity and therefore we visualize and attempt to realize certain positions in the body of Christ. But this is worldly wisdom for the wisdom of God is different. God's wisdom says you know you level of maturity. You do not have to envision it. Therefore, because you know, you have nothing to prove or achieve. You do not have to show men your capability in the body of Christ because you have nothing to prove. You do not need the praises of men for your capabilities because you already have the love of the Father, which is more than enough satisfaction. You do not have to work to achieve a goal because it is God that will place you into any and all levels of your achievement and not you. You just have to obediently perform what God request via his Living Water (his Holy Spirit). So meekness is possible because rather than being the leader showing your capabilities, you are a servant helping others. The attitude of the servant is different because the servant is at a different station in life. And yes you can be a servant even if you are the leader.

It is like a private in the Army that holds a masters degree serving under an officer that just got his GED. Time and time again, the private will see the errors of the officer and understands the ridiculousness of his orders, but remembers he is still the servant that must obey the officer's orders. So he humbly shares his knowledge only when allowed and always stands willing to obey even when he thinks the orders are erroneous. He is a servant. If you are also a leader, then you must have the helping obedient attitude of the private while you lead to be a servant leader.

Imagine being in a Church with a Pastor that from time to time errors in the Word because he lacks knowledge in the Word.

I Am Come To Bring Living Water

When you note an error, you must be humble and understand you are there to serve the Pastor and not to lead the Pastor. So pray for the Pastor and humbly offer scriptural truth when requested. Otherwise, hold your peace and let God do the work. In such a case, you will always feel you could do so much more for the Church, but keep in mind God has not place you in the position to do that task. Be meek and accept your servant status.

I define Meekness as understanding you are a servant to all and acting accordingly. That is true for all believers. Even if you are the Pastor and representative of God for a flock of believers, you are still a servant of the flock and need to humble yourself and display your meekness as a work of your belief (faith). You can be meek as long as you remember you are a servant.

The last fruit of Living Water, **temperance** (enkrateia), is also a personal characteristic of one changed by Christ rather than a characteristic of Christ within the believer. It means self control as a form of contentment. I know the use of the word contentment is strange to many bible students. But if you are to understand temperance to the point of being able to be tempered, then you must know the means of achieving temperance. I could spend a lot of time telling you how to maintain self control. But the problem is it will quickly become a learned behavior and never become a way of life. So I am purposely altering the definition to provide the means of changing your behavior for good.

While I was writing this, a song by the Williams Brothers was playing on the radio. The song said, "I am just nobody trying to tell everybody about somebody that can save their soul." Now the words of that song do not sound unusually to most believers. For we know God has always selected the poor, the underdog, or the rejected of society to confound the wise.

Blessed are the poor in spirit: for theirs is the kingdom of heaven. (Matthew 5:3)

Hearken, my beloved brethren, Hath not God chosen the poor of this world rich in faith, and heirs of the kingdom which he hath promised to them that love him? (James 2:5)

I Am Come To Bring Living Water

We may never fully understand why God selects the unexpected person, but he does. Consider how many great ministers of the Lord you know that were never formally trained in their profession or that obtained their training long after God selected or called them to their ministry. In many cases, these men and women of God only go to training to satisfy those of us that need to see their degrees to trust their wisdom. And how can they have this wisdom without training? It is because their wisdom comes from God and not from man.

So what is the secret to becoming tempered? The simple truth is you can have self control when you become completely content with what you are today. We become anxious, lustful, desirous, and even angry when we want things we do not have. We actually lust after those things. We are troubled to see others have those things and our whole being becomes inclined at achieving the goal of having those things at all cost. We are frustrated by our failure to achieve the goal. That frustration results in a warring spirit that will impact others around us. It starts as an internal battle within us and extends to everyone we contact that is not working to fulfill our own internal lust.

From whence come wars and fightings among you? come they not hence, even of your lusts that war in your members? Ye lust, and have not: ye kill, and desire to have, and cannot obtain: ye fight and war, yet ye have not, because ye ask not. Ye ask, and receive not, because ye ask amiss, that ye may consume it upon your lusts. Ye adulterers and adulteresses, know ye not that the friendship of the world is enmity with God? whosoever therefore will be a friend of the world is the enemy of God. Do ye think that the scripture saith in vain, The spirit that dwelleth in us lusteth to envy? (James 4:1-5)

So how do I overcome? Become content with what you have and the state you are in. Never lust for that you do not have and this war will never begin. Learn to temper your internal emotions and you will begin to display a personal characteristic of temperance. Let the Spirit of God show you your lust and reframe from the lust. Then God will provide you with the strength to be happy in what ever state you find yourself.

Well those are the fruits of Living Water (more commonly referred to as the fruit of the Spirit). Love, joy, peace and long-suffering are enabled because Christ is within me. It is the Christ within me that causes these fruits. Gentleness, goodness, faith, meekness and temperance are the results of having Christ change my life. They are the fruits I become because I am changed by Christ. Love, joy, peace and longsuffering are what you see in me because you see Christ within me and gentleness, goodness, faith, meekness, and temperance is are what I become when Christ changed my life and they are what you will experience from me.

Why do I Need Living Waters?

So why do I need Living Waters. I believed in Jesus. I have been cleansed by his blood. I have been baptized in water, washing away all my sins. So why do I need the Holy Ghost? I mean does the Holy Ghost add anything I have not already received? What if I am never baptized in the Holy Ghost, will I be blocked from entering Kingdom of God and the rest of the Lord?

These are great questions. I am not sure I will address each one, but there is evidence of why you need the Living Waters (Holy Spirit) I have not yet explained. And this evidence is why I believe God has commanded me to be a bearer of Living Waters. Like most truths of God it is very simple but frequently overlooked by so many.

This is he that came by water and blood, even Jesus Christ; not by water only, but by water and blood. And it is the Spirit that beareth witness, because the Spirit is truth. For there are three that bear record in heaven, the Father, the Word, and the Holy Ghost: and these three are one. And there are three that bear witness in earth, the Spirit, and the water, and the blood: and these three agree in one. If we receive the witness of men, the witness of God is greater: for this is the witness of God which he hath testified of his Son. (1 John 5:6-9)

With the coming of Jesus, the world was provided new critical sacraments. One of the new critical sacraments is water baptism for the remission or the cleansing of sins. John the Baptist introduced us to the sacrament and put it in place so Jesus could himself be baptized as the forerunner of our faith. Christ could not baptize himself, so John had to come first. Then just before Christ ministry was to end on earth, he sat down and instituted the Lord's Supper, a sacrament that reminds us he gave his life and shed his blood for the forgiveness of our sins. It was done near the end of his ministry because it required his giving his life to become effective. So it was one of the last lessons given to his disciples prior to his going to the cross. There were other new critical sacraments. One of which is key to this discussion. It is one many Christians today do not even recognize as a sacrament. It kind of slipped from our practices. It was a critical sacrament in the practice of the early Church and its believers, but for many of our churches it is rarely even discussed today. It was the decent of the Holy Spirit on Christ right after Jesus was baptized symbolizing the baptism of the Holy Ghost. Remember the Word spoken from heaven.

And Jesus, when he was baptized, went up straightway out of the water: and, lo, the heavens were opened unto him, and he saw the Spirit of God descending like a dove, and lighting upon him: And lo a voice from heaven, saying, This is my beloved Son, in whom I am well pleased. (Matthew 3:16-17)

What happened? The Holy Spirit bore witness Jesus is the son of God. "This is my beloved Son, in whom I am well pleased." So you have it, the water to clean away sins, the blood to provide forgiveness for sins, and the Holy Spirit (the Living Water) to bear witness of the son of God (the bread or Word of God). The three are on earth operating as one inside of you and me. Without the Holy Spirit, who will witness that you and I are changed? Who will speak and be heard on earth and in heaven that you and I are changed? Who will be able to search out ever muscle, bone, and fiber of our being and determine we have been change and are now become children of God?

It is so simple, in heaven just like there is God to declare Jesus is the son of God with the Holy Spirit bearing witness of the same, on earth, the cleaning water and the redeeming blood allow me to declare I am a child of God with the Holy Spirit bearing witness of the same. The Holy Spirit bears witness Jesus is the son of God in heaven. The Holy Spirit bears witness I am a child of God on earth. Now some of you may be pleased to live a life where men say you are a child of God. You know what I mean; your next door neighbor sees you going to church every Sunday and says you must be a Christian. As for me I prefer to have the witness of the Holy Spirit. I prefer to have the same one that witnessed Jesus was the Son of God also witness I am a child of

I Am Come To Bring Living Water

God. I prefer to have Living Water, the Spirit of God witness I am a child of God.

I know you are thinking that was not simple. Let me say it another way so you will understand the simplicity. While Jesus was walking the earth, his Father in heaven told people he was the son of God. It happened when he was born, when he was baptized, and when he was transfigured. God the Father, who is a Spirit, spoke from Heaven and proclaimed Jesus was his son and he was pleased with his son. We Christians on earth should want the same proclamation about us. We should want the Spirit of God declare us to be sons of God and joint heirs with Christ. So I need the Holy Spirit in my life so he may proclaim I am a child of God. If the Holy Spirit is not in me, he cannot make the claim. If he is within me, then he can claim to the world and to God almighty I am a child of God. It is that simple. So I need to drink this Living Water. Others also need to drink this Living Water. And that is why I am the bearer of Living Water. I am come to bring Living Water. The grass of a field, the lily of a valley and people will dry up and die without water. How much more so will your soul parish without the Living Water of life. I am not the creator of the Living Water and I am not the Living Water. I am just the bearer of the Living Water.

But whosoever drinketh of the water that I shall give him shall never thirst: but the water that I shall give him shall be in him a well of water springing up into everlasting life. (John 4:14)

I Am Come To Bring Living Water

Now give this book to another Christian and help change their walk in Christ with a drink of Living Water.

I Am Come To Bring Living Water

Darris L. Martin

In the Body of Christ

Darris Martin completed Able Ministry training at Gospel Crusade, Incorporated (a non denominational religious retreat, bible school, missionary and church) in Bradenton, FL. Darris was ordained by the same church. While Darris is a fully ordained minister, he prefers to remain in his calling as a bible teacher.

In the Community

Darris Martin has been active in most communities he has resided. Over the years the two most significant involvements were managing a pilot temporary housing facility for displaced individual under HUD in Daytona Beach, FL (these housing facilities are now available nation wide) and Treasurer of Homeland Charities, Incorporated (Homeland Charities is a U.S. 501-C3 non-profit organization that aims to alleviate the devastating impact of HIV/AIDS in Abia State, Nigeria. To meet this goal, Homeland has assembled collaborators, sponsors, endorsements, and resources that will provide comprehensive, innovative and cost-effective programs of Prevention, Treatment, and Research).

In the Work Place

Darris Martin is retired from Lockheed Martin after 37 years of service, where he last held the position of Electronics Systems Senior Quality Engineering Manager. He managed the implementation of several key corporate initiatives.

Darris has a Bachelors Degree from Indiana University in Business Finance. He resides in Pilesgrove, NJ.

I Am Come To Bring Living Water

www.ingramcontent.com/pod-product-compliance
Lightning Source LLC
LaVergne TN
LVHW011202080426
835508LV00007B/549